Patricia Wolfe

Brain Matters

Translating Research into Classroom Practice

Association for Supervision and Curriculum Development Alexandria, Virginia USA

®

Association for Supervision and Curriculum Development
1703 N. Beauregard St. • Alexandria, VA 22311-1714 USA
Telephone: 1-800-933-2723 or 703-578-9600 • Fax: 703-575-5400
Web site: http://www.ascd.org • E-mail: member@ascd.org

Printed in the United States of America.

Original illustrations in Chapters 2–4 copyright 2001 by Hunter Hollingsworth.

July 2001 member book (pc). ASCD Premium, Comprehensive, and Regular members periodically receive ASCD books as part of their membership benefits. No. FY01-08.

ASCD Product No. 101004
ASCD member price: $21.95   nonmember price: $25.95

Library of Congress Cataloging-in-Publication Data

Wolfe, Pat.
  Brain matters : translating research into classroom practice /
Patricia Wolfe.
      p. cm.
Includes bibliographical references (p.   ) and index.
  ISBN 0-87120-517-3 (alk. paper)
  1. Learning, Psychology of. 2. Learning—Physiological aspects. 3.
Brain. I. Title.
  LB1060 .W63 2001
  370.15'23—dc21
                              2001002013

06 05 04 03 02 01   10 9 8 7 6 5 4 3 2 1

Brain WITHDRAWN Matters

Translating Research into Classroom Practice

Preface and Acknowledgments

Some scientists and educators think it is too soon to apply brain research to the classroom, because we don't know enough yet. The field is so new, they say, and the discoveries in many cases so narrow in their focus, that we run the risk of making false assumptions and perhaps even dangerous applications.

On the one hand, their caution is warranted. Educators have a history of jumping on bandwagons, and they often have accepted unproven theories as fact and have applied strategies without careful analysis of their effectiveness. There is still a great deal we do not know about how the human brain functions. Neuroscience research is in its infancy, and new studies often refute the previous month's findings.

On the other hand, it would be foolish to wait until all the research is in and we have absolute certainty before beginning our study of the brain and discussing the possible implications and applications of research findings. Much of the research already confirms what experienced educators have long known and used in their classrooms. What the research adds, at this point, is a partial understanding of why certain procedures or strategies work. As a result, we no longer have to operate intuitively but can begin to articulate and explain the rationale for what we do. Madeline Hunter said that the problem with teaching intuitively is that intuition is sterile: It can't be passed on. For this reason, teachers have often had difficulty explaining their craft to others.

~ ~ ~

Another reason for educators to study the brain is that it is the focus of their daily work. Saying that we do not need to understand the brain to be able teach it, is like saying that a physician need not understand the body in order to treat it. In the past, people considered the brain a "black box," a mystery that defied comprehension. We could observe what went into it and what came out, but we had no understanding of the internal operations. Now that research is beginning to unlock the mysterious box, we would be imprudent to ignore the research and say it has no implications for teaching and learning. In fact, the better we understand the brain, the better we'll be able to educate it.

We also need a functional understanding of the brain and how it operates to be able to critically analyze the vast amount of neuroscientific information arriving almost daily. Some of this information is reported in depth and is reliable, while other findings have been reduced to "sound bites" that invite misinterpretation. If we are to receive full benefit from this information (and be viewed as professionals), we need to develop a solid knowledge base that reflects an accurate understanding of the research. But to read and understand the research findings, we need to be familiar with the procedures and protocols that were used, and we need to know about the structure and function of the brain. We do not have to become scientific experts, but we do need to look critically at the sources of the information. Too often, the media report "facts" about brain functioning on the basis of one small study or, worse, from poorly conducted studies. This results in what we might call pseudoscience, statements that often begin with, "Research proves . . . ," when in actuality the study needs to be replicated in a variety of situations or with other subjects before it can be considered valid or reliable.

I am neither a neuroscientist nor a researcher in the technical sense of the words. I have spent my entire career teaching students at nearly every grade level and, for the past 20 years, working with teachers at nearly every grade level and subject area. My interest in brain research began in the early 1980s when I was a staff developer conducting workshops on effective teaching strategies. In searching for ways to understand why some strategies worked and others didn't, I began to find bits of information from sources that mentioned studies on the brain and how it acquires and stores data. This was exciting! Imagine having some scientific data to back up the classroom activities we were sharing with teachers.

~ ~ ~

But it wasn't quite as simple as I had imagined. First, the studies were difficult to locate; and when I found them, the language in which they were written was nearly foreign to me. I had no functional understanding of the brain, so the terms used had little meaning. Second, none of the research said anything about practical applications outside the medical field, let alone specific information about how the findings might apply to the field of education. It was several years before I found a book that discussed brain research in nonscientific terms, *The 3-Pound Universe* by Hooper and Teresi (1986). Today, my library contains nearly 100 books on the brain, many written for the general public by neuroscientists and some that actually discuss the learning process. There truly has been an explosion of information about the brain and a corresponding explosion of interest in it.

Although most people seem to be fascinated with information about how their brains work, teachers have probably shown the strongest interest in the research. For here at last may be answers to some of the problems we've struggled with for so long: Why do some students learn to read so quickly and others have such a difficult time figuring out the process? How can students sit through an excellent lesson on Monday, and on Tuesday act as if they have never heard the information before? Why are some seemingly simple concepts so difficult for some students to grasp, while others have no trouble with them? What causes attention deficit hyperactivity disorder (ADHD) or autism, and how can we help students with these and other disorders?

We still don't have all the answers to these questions, but we are getting closer; and the possibility of having a better base of information about the teaching/learning process is something that educators long for. Although we are not scientists or researchers, we do work in the laboratory called a classroom, and we have a tremendous amount of knowledge and understanding of the teaching/learning process. We have gained this knowledge through experience and from research in educational psychology, cognitive psychology, and teaching methodology. It is up to us to decide how the research from all these sources best informs our practice.

Though I have tried to be accurate in my explanations, they are my own understanding of a complex subject. The implications and applications are (with a few exceptions) of my own creation, based on my own experience and my understanding of the research. This book does not address *all* the fascinating information about the brain; I have selected only those aspects of the research that I think have the most import for educators.

~ ~ ~

This book also contains more caveats than definitive answers, because the field is so new and not all neuroscientists agree on the findings. I believe, however, that focusing staff development on the results of brain research will not only stimulate further interest and study, but will also provide a newer framework for understanding the complex and difficult job of teaching the human brain.

The book is divided into three parts. Part I is a minitextbook on brain-imaging techniques and the anatomy and physiology of the brain. This part contains some rather technical areas, and readers may choose to skim it first, then refer back to it as needed when reading the rest of the book. (The glossary at the back of this book lists and defines terms that may be unfamiliar to some readers.) Part II introduces a model of how the brain processes information and explores some of the implications of this process for classroom practice. Part III presents examples of teaching strategies that match how the brain learns best, through projects, simulations, visuals, music, writing, and mnemonics.

Many people have contributed to what I know and have written in this book. Madeline Hunter was my master teacher, my friend, and my mentor; she helped me understand that there is both a science and an art to teaching. Marian Diamond has shared her vast knowledge and wisdom and challenged me to read analytically and write accurately. Teachers from around the world have generously shared their practices and strategies with me. I am grateful to master teachers Marie Bañuelos, Jean Blaydes, Belinda Borgaard, Joan Carlson, Marilyn Hrycauk, Alice Jackson, James Johnson, Brian Jones, Ellen Ljung, Mary Martin, Ted Migdal, Janet Mendelsohn, Jane Politte, Bonnie Shouse, Ramona Smith, Marny Sorgen, Janet Steinman, Anne Westwater, and Alan Fisk-Williams, all of whose strategies appear in this book.

This book would never have been written if not for Ron Brandt; Joyce McLeod, my development editor at ASCD; and Bob Sylwester, who convinced me I could write even though I was certain I could not. I am very grateful for their encouragement, expert feedback, and support; they have been the best of coaches. If this book is readable, the credit must also be shared with Anne Westwater, Terry Thatcher, and John Wheeler. They unselfishly read every word of the book, provided invaluable feedback on content and style, and helped me get the commas in the right places.

PART I

The Structure and Function of the Human Brain

The more we understand the brain, the better we'll be able to design instruction to match how it learns best.

The human brain is not the largest organ in the body. It weighs only about 3 pounds, less than the skin covering your body. Yet this marvelous structure is the source of all human behavior, simultaneously controlling a myriad of unbelievably complex functions. Within a span of time too short for humans to measure, it receives information and relays it to the appropriate locations for processing. It then allows you to act on these data by controlling the motor output of your muscles. Your brain generates emotions and lets you be aware of them. It is the source of cognition, memory, thoughts, and what we call intelligence. Your ability to speak and understand the speech of others comes from the brain. You don't have to worry about controlling your heart rate, respiration, breathing, hormone secretion, or immune system; the brain does this for you unconsciously and automatically.

In Part I we'll take a look at the major structures of the brain and the roles they play.

You may be wondering why you need all this biology. Wouldn't it be sufficient just to outline the general findings about how the brain learns without understanding the structures involved? Isn't it possible to have a general understanding of research findings and perhaps even apply the findings without really comprehending what is going on in the brain? Perhaps, but I believe that if we are to become critical consumers of neuroscience and cognitive science research, or even to read reports of the research in the media with any understanding, we need to have a working knowledge of the human brain. Leslie Hart (1983) in his book *Human Brain, Human Learning*, talks about how little sense it would make to design a device to be used by human hands without being sure that you considered the nature of hands. Neither should we consider designing instruction to teach the human brain without taking into account the brain and how it functions. The more we understand the brain, the better we'll be able to design instruction to match how it learns best. Let us begin our exciting journey into the amazing universe within.

Opening the Black Box of the Brain

Introduction

We've learned more about the brain and how it functions in the past two decades than in all of recorded history. What is largely responsible for this explosion of information? The answer lies largely in improved technology. Many years ago the only way brains could be studied was by the initially illegal method of autopsy. And while studying the brain after death provided an enormous amount of information—delineating the areas that allow us to produce and interpret speech, for example—it did little to increase our understanding of how information is processed and stored or why certain students have difficulty learning how to read. Today, imaging techniques allow us to look at the specific brain areas a person uses when recalling a noun versus a verb, or when listening to music versus composing a song. We literally can look inside a brain and see which areas are most active while the person is engaged in various mental activities.

We literally can look inside a brain and see which areas are most active while the person is engaged in various mental activities.

The chronology of brain imaging includes many methodologies that, although older and more primitive, remain viable today. As mentioned, the first method was autopsy, which has been in use since the days of da Vinci and is still useful. Scientists have learned a great deal about what causes Alzheimer's Disease, for example, by studying the brain tissue of those who died of this disease. Scientists have also learned much about the link between structure and function by studying people who have had brain injuries, strokes, or other traumas.

Animal studies have long been used to increase our understanding of how the brain works. This is possible because all mammalian brains function in a similar manner. Even though many of the methods used with animals cannot be applied to human subjects, we will see later that these studies often are useful to increase our understanding of human brain functioning.

Brain Imaging Techniques

X-Rays

The journey to the present "electronic age" of imaging techniques began with the development of the x-ray, discovered in 1895. X-rays are high-frequency electromagnetic waves that easily penetrate nonmetallic objects. When they do, the atoms in the test object absorb some of the radiation, leaving the unabsorbed portion to strike and expose a photographic plate. The more dense objects show up lighter on the plate, while the less dense objects look darker. Although this process works well if we want to see whether a bone is broken (or what objects you are carrying in your luggage at the airport), it is of little use in depicting the brain and other parts of the body that are largely composed of soft tissue with little contrast in density between areas.

Computerized Axial Tomography (CAT) Scans

In the early 1970s, a technique was developed to increase the gradations in shades of grey from the approximately 25 of the normal x-ray to more than 200. This procedure is called computerized axial tomography (CAT) scanning. It uses x-ray technology but combines several two-dimensional images into a set of three-dimensional "slices." The images resulting from a CAT scan look like a greyish x-ray but give a much clearer and more detailed picture of the brain. Neurologists and neurosurgeons routinely use these pictures to locate and determine the extent of tumors or lesions and the loss of tissue. As sophisticated and useful as they are, however, x-ray and CAT scans do not address the issue of function, which is the primary concern of those of us whose job is to understand the learning process.

The resting brain uses oxygen and glucose at 10 times the rate of the rest of the body.

Monitoring the Brain's Energy Consumption

To understand how some of the newer imaging techniques work, we need a little background information on the use of energy by the brain. Your brain is the "greediest" organ in the body. The resting brain uses oxygen and glucose at 10 times the rate of the rest of the body. Thus, even though the brain makes up less than 2.5 percent of total body weight, it is responsible for 20 percent of the body's energy consumption. The major sources of energy for the brain are oxygen and glucose, a simple carbohydrate. When certain areas of the brain are active, cells in those areas have a greater need for glucose and oxygen. Scientists realized that if they could trace the flow and consumption of either of these substances in the brain, they could tell which areas were working the hardest and therefore were responsible for a certain action. Around 1973, they began working to develop instruments that could construct an image of the brain by measuring the emissions given off as oxygen and glucose were consumed. Positron Emission Tomography (PET) and Magnetic Resonance Imaging (MRI) are two of the resulting brain-imaging methods. Figure 1.1 shows a comparison of three images of a slice of brain obtained by CAT, PET, and MRI.

Brain
Matters: Translating Research into Classroom Practice

Starting at 9 o'clock in the figure and moving clockwise are images obtained with standard photography, x-ray CAT, PET (most often created in color), and MRI.

Positron Emission Tomography (PET) Scans

PET is one of the most exciting advances in brain imaging. This technique allows scientists to picture the anatomical areas that become active while a person performs various mental tasks. The subject is injected with a small amount of radioactive

---

~ Figure 1.1 ~
IMAGING TECHNIQUES

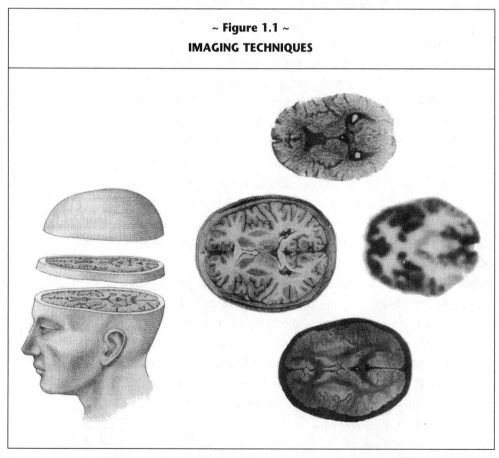

Source: Gregory, R. (Ed.). (1987). *The Oxford companion to the mind.* New York: Oxford University Press, p. 348. Reproduced by permission, courtesy of Drs. Michael E. Phelps, Edward J. Hoffman, and John C. Mazziotta, UCLA School of Medicine.

glucose, which the blood carries to the brain. The subject is placed in a PET scanner and asked to engage in a series of mental activities such as listening to words, saying words, or generating words. Subjects are given a noun and must generate a verb that they associate with that noun. The brain areas responsible for these various activities will use much more of the radioactive glucose than other areas. When this happens, the radioactive material emits antimatter particles called positrons, which collide with the brain's electrons and produce gamma rays. These gamma rays travel through the skull and can be detected by sensors outside the head. From this information, a computer constructs colored images (tomographs). The areas of the highest glucose use and, therefore, of greatest activity show up in white, red, and yellow, while areas of lesser use glow as green, blue, and purple (Posner & Raichle, 1997, p. 18).

PET does have several drawbacks. For one thing, because it requires the injection of a radioactive tracer, a person is generally allowed only one scanning session (usually 12 scans) a year. For another, neurons fire in milliseconds, but it requires about 40 seconds to obtain the data necessary to build an image of activity with PET. Therefore, how long an area remains active and the sequence of the activation of neural networks is not captured with this methodology. Third, while a PET scan gives an excellent picture of overall activity in the brain, it does not show the specific area in which the activity is occurring.

Functional Magnetic Resonance Imaging (fMRI) Technology

fMRI is one of the newest brain-imaging techniques to address some of PET's shortcomings. To understand how it works, we must first look at the basic MRI technology. A large part of the human body is water, which is made of magnetically polarized molecules. An MRI takes advantage of the fact that the hydrogen atoms in the body's water can be made to behave like tiny magnets if they are placed in a strong magnetic field. A beam of radio waves fired from the MRI scanner will make the molecules of water in the body resonate and give off radio signals of their own. These waves are detected by sensors, and the information is then assembled into an image by a computer (Greenfield, 1997). The imaging of specific organs by this technique far surpasses the detail produced by CAT because the spatial resolution is much finer. In brain research, MRI is used widely to locate tumors and lesions, or to identify other areas of abnormalities.

The primary goal of fMRI is to show not only structures of the brain but also neural activity. First used in England in 1986, fMRI scanning in the United States has expanded over the past few years, partly because MRI scanners now are widely available and partly because they are much less expensive than PET scanners.

fMRI works much like a standard MRI. The subject is asked to engage in an activity such as tapping a finger or listening to a sound. The parts of the brain that are responsible for these activities will cause certain neurons to fire. These neural impulses require energy, so more blood flows to these regions. The oxygen in the blood changes the magnetic field so that the radio signal emitted becomes more intense. The fMRI scanner detects and measures these changes in intensity and produces a computer image. By subtracting this image from an image of the brain at rest, the computer produces a detailed picture of the brain activity responsible for moving a finger or listening to a tone. The scanner produces a rapid series of images, which result in a sort of "movie" of brain activity. The latest scanners can produce four images every second. The human brain reacts to a stimulus in about half a second, so the rapid scanning of fMRI can clearly show the ebb and flow of activity in various parts of the brain as it reacts to different stimuli or undertakes different tasks. A powerful fMRI can thus assemble a functional image of an entire brain in two to six seconds, compared with one minute for a PET scan. In addition, the fMRI can be repeated within seconds, while PET takes nine minutes for the radiation to dissipate (Carter, 1998). fMRI is also less invasive than PET because it does not require the introduction of a radioactive substance into the body.

Electroencephalography (EEG)

Even though the speed of fMRI scanning is impressive, this technique cannot capture the much faster fluctuations in electrical activity that occur as neurons communicate with one another. In order to follow the moment-to-moment changes in neuronal activity, the scientists must turn to other methods such as EEG.

EEG is an imaging tool that has been in use for more than half a century. It measures electrical patterns created by the oscillations of neurons. On an ongoing basis, even during sleep, these electrical signals are constantly flashing throughout the brain. The tissues of the body conduct electricity well, so that sensors placed on the scalp can detect the impulses passing from the brain through the skull and the scalp. The electroencephalograph amplifies the signals and records them on a monitor or paper chart. You are probably familiar with the term *brain waves*, the name given to these various patterns of electrical activity.

Brain-wave frequency is measured by recording the number of cycles or oscillations per second. The more oscillations per second, the higher the frequency of the wave. During wakefulness, the waves are small and fast and are called alpha waves. Oscillations at the highest frequency, beta waves, occur during attention (beta I waves) and intense mental activity (beta II waves). When we become drowsy and enter into light sleep, the waves slow down and are called theta waves. Entering into deep sleep produces large, slow waves known as delta waves.

Electroencephalography has provided a valuable tool for both researchers and clinicians, especially in the fields of epilepsy and sleep physiology, but it is also used in education-related issues such as language processing. Paula Tallal, language expert at Rutgers University, has used EEG along with MRI to determine that children with normal language skills have "lopsided" brains; that is, the left hemisphere is larger and more active than the right. This makes sense, since we know that in most people the left hemisphere specializes in language processing and the production of speech. Tallal has discovered, however, that the brains of children with language disorders often have balanced brains with both left and right hemispheres nearly equal in size and activity. She determined that the underpowered left hemisphere was not fast enough to adequately process language at normal speeds. A program, Fast Forward, developed by Tallal and Michael Merzenich at the University of California, San Francisco, has been successful in speeding up the processing levels in many children with this brain-based language delay (Tallal, 2000).

On the Horizon

Several newer imaging techniques promise to give us even more detailed pictures of the brain and how it functions. Among these are single-photon emission computerized tomography (SPECT), near-infrared-spectroscopy (NIRS), and magnetoencephalography (MEG). Multimodal imaging, which combines two or more techniques, is becoming increasingly popular.

Research is in progress to see whether neural differences exist between dyslexics and non-impaired readers (Shaywitz, 1999). Another area of great concern, to parents as well as teachers, is attention deficit hyperactivity disorder (ADHD). Early studies support the idea that an underlying neurological dysfunction is linked to the behaviors of children and adults with this disorder. Attempts to understand autism, eating disorders, obsessive-compulsive disorder (OCD), and other problems that affect students' school performance are the focus of numerous current neuroscientific studies.

Interpreting Brain Imaging for Educational Purposes

Will the day come when educators will have ready access to brain-imaging machines to assist them in diagnosing reading or attention problems? It may not be too outrageous to think so. But until that happens, our best bet is to educate ourselves about how these various methodologies work and to understand what they can and cannot do for us. Rarely does neuroscience prove that a particular classroom strategy works, but the information coming from the neurosciences certainly can provide a more informed basis for the decisions we make in our schools and classrooms.

For example, PET scans of a reader show that much more frontal lobe activity occurs when the subject reads silently than when he or she is reading aloud to others. Activity in the frontal lobes often indicates higher-level thinking. On the other hand, the scan of the student reading aloud glows brightly in the motor area of the brain that governs speech, while showing little activity elsewhere. One way to interpret these scans is that there is more comprehension of what is being read when one reads silently. Do these scans prove that students should never read aloud? Of course they don't. Armed with this information, however, teachers are able to make more informed decisions about how to balance silent and oral reading to obtain both diagnostic information on decoding problems and how to enhance comprehension of what is being read.

Synapse Strengtheners

1. Skim back over this chapter, then close the book and see if you can explain the major differences between a PET scan and an fMRI scan.

2. If you are reading this book as part of a study group, ask each person in the group to identify one common student learning problem and speculate which brain-imaging technique might provide the most information toward understanding the problem and why.

3. Using the diagram of the scans in Figure 1.1, explain to someone who has not read the book how these images were obtained and what they show.

4. Explain how the new brain-imaging techniques affect our thinking about educational practice but do not necessarily prove that certain strategies work.

Brain Anatomy—A Short Course: Neurons and Subcortical Structures

2

I magine that you are pushing a grocery cart in the produce section of your local supermarket. As you see yourself walking down the wide, well-lit aisle, visualize the neatly ordered bins, each containing a different fruit or vegetable. Can you see the vivid dark purple of the eggplant? Can you smell the ripe peaches? Imagine yourself reaching the bin containing the cabbages. Pick up a big solid head and place it in the hanging scale. You read the numbers on the scale and see that your head of cabbage weighs about 3 pounds.

Your ability to mentally reproduce the above scenario—complete with all the sights, tactile sensations, smells, and sounds—is the result of the interaction of millions of neurons in a brain weighing about the same as that large head of cabbage. Isn't this an amazing organ that allows you not only to experience the world outside its bony casing, but also to be aware of and discuss the experiences? To start to understand it, let's begin our tour of the human brain by looking at its basic structural and functional unit, the cell.

Starting at the Beginning: The Cells

The entire body is composed of cells. The muscles, lining of the intestines, bones, skin, and brain are all made up of billions of these basic units. Each cell or group of cells has a specific job to perform. The cells that constitute the central nervous system (CNS) comprise the brain and the spinal cord; along with the endocrine system, they provide most of the control functions for the body. Two types of cells make up the CNS: neurons and glial cells. Let's look first at the basic functional unit of the CNS, the neuron.

Neurons

Neurons, found primarily in the brain and in the spinal cord (the central nervous system), number approximately 100 billion. They differ from most of the other cells in the body in two major ways. First, they do not appear to regenerate on a regular, programmed basis, as do most other cells. Nearly all the cells in your body (skin cells, blood cells, the cells that form the lining of your stomach) continually renew themselves every few days or months. This is why your skin heals when you cut yourself and why when you break a leg, the fracture will usually mend if the bone is set correctly. But if neurons are destroyed through a stroke or other trauma, they do not regenerate in the same manner. But there's news on this horizon. We have long believed that humans are born with all the neurons they will ever have. Recent research is challenging this dogma. Several studies have shown that the adult brain does generate new neurons, although the process by which this happens and how these new cells function is not yet fully understood (Gould, Reeves, Graziano, & Gross, 1999; Kempermann & Gage, 1999).

The second way neurons differ from other types of cells is in their ability to transmit information. Neurons "communicate" with one another and form networks by means of electrical and chemical signals. To do this, they need a different design from other cells, which is the third way in which they are different. In Greek, the word neuron means "string." In Figure 2.1 you can see how this unusual-looking cell got its name.

Neurons come in several different shapes. Some are shaped like a pyramid, and others look something like a giant sea fan. Regardless of their shape, most neurons are composed of a cell body, or *soma*, which contains the nucleus, thousands of short

~ Figure 2.1 ~
THE NEURON

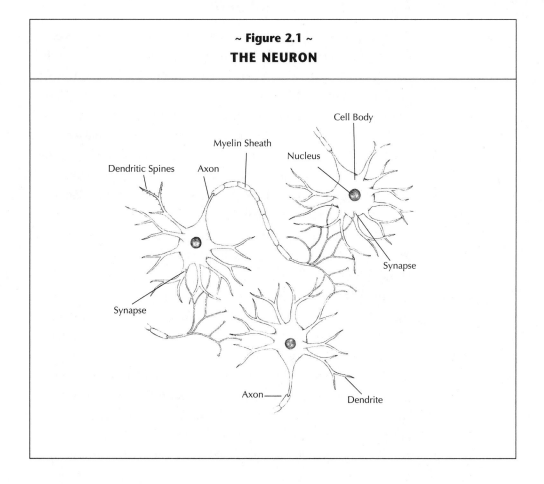

projections called dendrites (from the Greek word for tree, *dendra*), and a single axon, which is usually covered by a fatty substance called myelin. Dendrites *receive* information from other cells. The main job of the axon is to *send* information to other cells. The end of the axon splits into branches, each of which ends in an axon terminal or bulb. Neurons communicate electrochemically by passing messages at the junction (known as the synapse) between axon terminals and spines on dendrites or cell bodies.

Prenatal Development of Neurons

From conception to birth, an amazing process takes place called neurogenesis, or development of the nervous system. It is during this time that (1) neurons are generated from undifferentiated stem cells; (2) the neurons migrate from the site where they were generated to their final positions; (3) the neurons aggregate into distinct brain regions; and (4) neurons begin to make connections among one another. If a child's brain contains approximately 100 billion neurons at birth, and it already has made trillions of connections, then it stands to reason that the fetal brain has been busy producing all those cells.

In the embryonic brain, cells divide to generate new neurons at the astonishing rate of 250,000 per minute! (Cowan, 1979). Hundreds of billions of neurons are created—many more, we will see, than are needed. Next, in a process known as migration, the neurons travel to their designated places by aggregating into layers, clusters, and tracts, forming the myriad structures that make up the brain. As soon as this happens, the cells start forming random synaptic connections, again more than are needed. If neurons fail to form enough synaptic contact points or migrate to the wrong place, they are pruned away in a process known as *apoptosis*, or programmed cell death. In her book, *Magic Trees of the Mind*, researcher and neuroanatomist Marian Diamond

In the embryonic brain, cells divide to generate new neurons at the astonishing rate of 250,000 per minute!

estimates that approximately 50 percent of the neurons that have been generated are pared away before birth by this natural cell death (Diamond, Hopson, & Diamond, 1998). The purpose of apoptosis seems to be not only to eliminate neurons that don't make the right connections, but also to strengthen the connections that are left and perhaps prevent the brain from becoming "overstuffed" with its own cells. Incomplete apoptosis may account for the astonishing abilities of savants, as well as being a causal factor in their deficiencies in other areas (Carter, 1998).

After brain cells have been created, have migrated, and have been "pruned," the neurons spontaneously start firing without any external stimuli, making connections and, in a sense, trying out their circuits to make certain that they work. Again a pruning process will take place, although this time it is a whittling away of connections, not neurons. It isn't until the beginning of the third trimester that the fetus's sensory organs begin to mature enough to react to stimuli outside the womb. Susan Greenfield notes in her book, *The Human Brain*, that it is also around seven months *in utero* that the convolutions begin to appear in the outer covering of the brain (Greenfield, 1997). At this point the fetus responds to detectable light levels and to sound. Yes, the fetus "learns" before birth! A baby is born able to distinguish its mother's voice and odor from others, and can even recognize music it heard before it was born (Davis, 1997).

Glial Cells

As amazing as the formation of neurons and their networks is, this process could not take place without the assistance of the helper cells in the brain, the glial cells, also known as neuroglia. The term "glia" is derived from the Greek word meaning "glue," which reflects a mistaken assumption that these cells in some way held the neurons together. Glial cells, which outnumber neurons 10 to 1, are quite different from neurons. The major distinction is that they do not participate directly in electrical signaling as neurons do, although some of their supporting functions help in the process.

One of the primary roles that glial cells play is in the development of the fetal brain. Some of these cells, the radial glia, physically travel from their point of origin ahead of neurons and form a temporary scaffolding for neurons to climb. Special adhesion molecules on the glial cells guide the neurons as they migrate to their predetermined place in one of the six layers of the cortex, the outer covering of the brain (discussed in more detail later in this chapter). According to Arnold Scheibel, former director of the Brain Research Institute at the University of California, Los Angeles, the migration process can go awry and may produce conditions that show up later in the child's development such as certain kinds of epilepsy, dyslexia, and perhaps schizophrenia (Scheibel, 2000).

Another type of glial cell, the macrophage, assists in removing the debris of dead cells following damage to brain areas. Still other glial cells, the oligodendrocytes, play a role in neural maturation, determining when neurons are ready to function efficiently. These cells lay down myelin, a laminated wrapping around some (but not all) axons, which speeds the electrical impulse down these extensions. Myelin is light in color and accounts for what is commonly known as the "white matter" of the brain.

A fourth type of glial cell, the astrocyte, is the most abundant glial cell in the brain. Astrocytes have a star-like appearance, and their main job is to maintain an appropriate chemical environment around the neuron. They act as a sort of sponge for mopping up potentially toxic chemicals. Astrocytes also play a role in keeping certain substances from brain tissue by helping to form and maintain the blood-brain barrier.

Central Nervous System Structures That Operate at the Unconscious Level

A simplified look at the brain would reveal two major divisions: (1) a relatively small subcortical system that operates at an unconscious level, processing basic survival tasks, and (2) a much larger cortex that processes the conscious decisions and responses we make to novel situations not covered by the subcortical systems. The structures under the cortex alert us to a danger or opportunity, while the cortex selects the most appropriate response strategy. As we look at the brain and how it functions, we will see how interconnected these two systems are. But first, let's look at the individual structures that make up these two major divisions.

Early in the brain's development, neurons begin to aggregate into regions. In the four-week-old embryo, the human brain is a series of bulges at one end of a neural tube. These bulges develop into three hindbrain regions, one midbrain area, and two forebrain areas. From these six divisions will develop the 40 or so major structures of the brain as well as all the smaller nuclei, ganglia, nerves, pathways, and canals that are essential for the CNS to function normally. (The actual number of structures depends on how you organize them. The visual system alone processes 30 tasks, and the cortex has been divided into 104 regions called Brodman Areas.) Let's look at the lowermost part of the CNS, the spinal cord. Each of the following structures is shown in Figure 2.2.

The chief job of the spinal cord is to carry messages between the brain and the body.

Spinal Cord

Running from the base of the brain down to the middle of the back is a large bundle of nerve fibers about 18 inches long (in

Brain
Matters: Translating Research into Classroom Practice

an adult) and slightly thinner than an index finger: the spinal cord. Structurally, the spinal cord is an extension of the brain. During embryonic development, both develop from the same neural tube, with the brain forming from the top of the tube and the spinal cord from the lower portion.

The chief job of the spinal cord is to carry messages between the brain and the body. It does this by way of two major corticospinal tracts, the ascending pathway and the descending pathway. The ascending pathway takes in sensory information, such

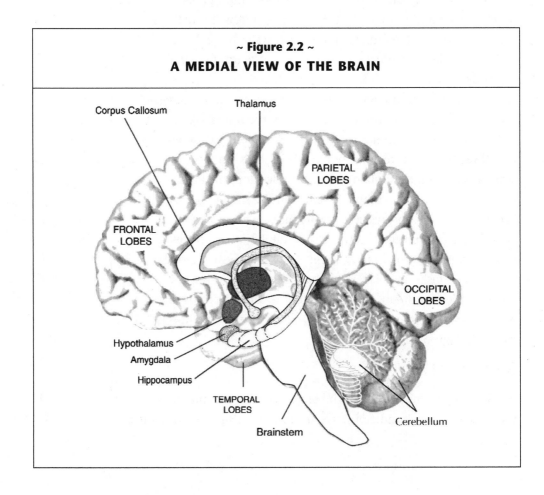

~ Figure 2.2 ~
A MEDIAL VIEW OF THE BRAIN

Corpus Callosum
Thalamus
PARIETAL LOBES
FRONTAL LOBES
OCCIPITAL LOBES
Hypothalamus
Amygdala
Hippocampus
TEMPORAL LOBES
Cerebellum
Brainstem

as pain, temperature, light, and touch from the body's sensory receptors and relays it to the specific brain regions that process these different types of sensations. This pathway also carries sensory messages about the position of joints and muscles to the brain stem for unconscious assessment of body position and posture. The descending pathway works in the opposite direction, carrying motor nerve signals from the brain to the body's muscles to cause movement.

The spinal cord is also able to carry out some reflex actions on its own, independent of the brain. Examples of reflexes are the knee jerk and pulling a hand away from a hot stove. The importance of the spinal cord is strikingly evident when damage to the cord occurs through either injury or disease. Depending on the location and severity of the damage, the effects can range from weakness in the extremities to total paralysis, loss of reflexes, and loss of sensation (Greenfield, 1996).

Brainstem

The brainstem, located at the base of the brain where the spinal cord begins, is one of the oldest parts of the brain in terms of evolution. It is made up of three main parts: the midbrain (upper end), the pons (center area), and the medulla oblongata (lower end). The brainstem is sometimes referred to as the reptilian brain, probably because its basic structure is rather like the entire brain of present-day reptiles. Given this fact, it isn't difficult to guess that its primary purpose is survival. The brainstem is largely in control of autonomic functions, those functions not under our conscious control, but essential for our survival. The necessity of the unconscious workings of the brainstem is obvious if you consider what your life would be like if you had to consciously control your breathing, heartbeat, and blood pressure— you would be able to do little else.

The necessity of the unconscious nature of the workings of the brainstem is obvious if you consider what your life would be like if you had to consciously control your breathing, heartbeat, or blood pressure; you would be able to do little else.

The brainstem accomplishes these feats by means of a network of neurons and fibers known as the reticular formation (RF), which occupies the core of the brain stem. The RF receives information from all over your body. Every time your body moves, some adjustment of heart rate, blood pressure, or breathing rate is needed to compensate for the changes that have occurred. The cells in the RF are in charge of regulating these basic life-support systems. In addition to controlling these vital systems, the RF contains other cells that control some eyeball movements, pupil constriction, stomach reflexes, facial expression, salivation, and taste. The RF is fairly mature at birth; a newborn's brain stem is already functioning to regulate the heart rate, blood pressure, and respiration (Diamond, Hopson, & Diamond, 1998).

An equally important function of the reticular system is the control of awareness levels. The RF, neurons in the thalamus, and other neurons from various sensory systems of the brain make up the reticular activating system (RAS). This system receives input from the body and changes the level of cell excitation to meet the changing conditions in the environment. For example, if stimulation is decreased by cutting down sensory input, such as putting a person in a dark, quiet room, the RAS decreases the level of excitation in the cortex and the level of consciousness is changed; the person may actually go to sleep. When the body awakens from sleep, the RAS increases the level of excitation in the cortex and the person becomes aware, or conscious (Binney & Janson, 1990). But whether we are drowsy, asleep, awake, hypervigilant, or unconscious, the activity of the brain stem continues to keep the life-support systems functioning. Severe damage to the RAS can result in a permanent coma.

The RAS also serves as an effective filter for the thousands of stimuli constantly bombarding the sensory receptors, allowing you to focus on relevant stimuli. It excludes background information and "tunes out" distractions or trivial sensory information, such as awareness of your clothes on your body or the feeling of your back against a chair. It is the RAS that allows you to fall asleep on a plane but to awake suddenly when the plane's engines change pitch.

A final, important role of the brainstem is in the production of many of the brain's chemical messengers. These chemicals come from nuclei (close-knit groups of nerve cell bodies) located in the brainstem and are projected widely to all other parts of the brain. We'll look more closely at their function in a later chapter.

Although it might appear that the functioning of the brainstem, and especially the RAS, is rather primitive and less important than more complex structures such as the large cerebral hemispheres with their intellectual capacities, this is not true. In fact, because it is a rather small structure, damage to the brainstem is highly life threatening, whereas damage to the much larger cortex may have relatively minor consequences, depending on the location and extent of the damage (Gazzaniga, Ivry, & Mangun, 1998). You could say that this small area of the brain holds the key to life itself.

Cerebellum

Moving up in the system, we encounter the cerebellum at the back of the brain. Its name is derived from Latin and means "little brain." It is a two-lobed, deeply folded structure overlaying the top of the brain stem, just under the occipital lobes, in the posterior portion of the brain. The cerebellum, like the brainstem, is primitive in evolutionary terms and has changed little over thousands of years.

In all mammals, the cerebellum is the key to balance, maintenance of body posture, and coordination of muscle function. Because humans have an almost unlimited repertoire of movement, the cerebellum is large, accounting for 11 percent of the brain's weight. From birth to age 2, the cerebellum grows faster

In all mammals the cerebellum is the key to coordination of balance, maintenance of body posture, and coordination of muscle actions.

than does the cerebral cortex. By age 2, it has almost reached its adult size (Binney & Janson, 1990). During this early period, the child is learning the basic movements, such as walking and grasping. The cerebellum stores these movement patterns in neural networks and then, throughout life, calls upon them whenever they are needed.

Coordinated movements, such as walking, lifting a glass, or writing a word, are activities that we often take for granted. The acquisition of the skilled movements involved in these activities begins under the conscious control of the cortex. Though the cortex can plan and initiate movements, it does not have the neural circuitry needed to calculate the sequences of muscular contractions necessary for the movements. That task falls to the cerebellum. When the cerebellum receives information (in about one-50th of a second) that the motor cortex has begun to initiate a movement, it computes the contribution that various muscles will have to make to perform that movement and sends the appropriate messages to those muscles. The action has begun.

Throughout the action, the cerebellum continuously monitors and modifies the activity in the muscles, making the changes necessary for smooth completion of the action. These complex maneuvers are also necessary when a person is sitting or standing. Information comes into the cerebellum not only from the motor cortex, spinal cord, and muscles, but also from the organs of balance in the vestibular area of the brain. This allows the cerebellum to continually modify activity in the motor pathways essential for maintaining the body in an upright position.

If you ever learned to drive a car, play the piano, or touch type, you probably remember what a long, laborious process it was and how many hours of practice it took to become proficient. If you still do any one of these today, it is likely that you do it so unconsciously you would have difficulty telling someone how you do it. You can thank your cerebellum for this ability.

What happens over time as the movements involved in playing the piano or driving the car are repeated over and over? We all know from our own experience that the skill becomes more and more automatic and that less conscious thought is needed to accomplish the task. (Have you ever driven your car over a familiar route, arrived at your destination, and realized that you were not aware of having driven there?) The brain allows us to engage in complex motor activities with almost no conscious awareness of the task.

With proficiency, the cerebellum takes over much of the control, leaving the conscious mind free to do and think about other things. How this occurs is not totally understood, although scientists have advanced several theories. One neurobiologist, W. T. Thach, from the University of Washington School of Medicine, suggests that the cerebellum may link a behavioral context to a motor response. He proposes that, as you practice a motor response (such as riding a bicycle) over and over, the occurrence of the context (getting on the bicycle) triggers the occurrence of the response (riding the bicycle) (Thach, 1996). In other words, the linkages between the motor areas of the cortex and the cerebellum permit an experiential context to automatically evoke an action.

Recently, researchers have also become interested in the functions of the cerebellum that do not deal specifically with motor functions. Blood flow and anatomical studies have shown close links between the frontal cortex and the cerebellum. Perhaps we'll find that the cerebellum plays a role in cognition (such as planning or imagining movements), as well as in the movements themselves.

Thalamus and Hypothalamus

Deep within the core of the brain, just above the brainstem, are two walnut-sized structures that play a critical role in regulating perception and the body's vital functions. The thalamus is a small plum-shaped structure located in the center of the brain. (You actually have two of them joined by a sort of bridge, but as with most duplicate structures in the brain, they are commonly referred to in the singular.) Named for the Greek word for "chamber" or "inner room," this brain structure is in a strategic position to act as a relay station to direct the flow of information between the sense organs and the cortex. It has been called the "gateway" to the cortex, because nearly all input from the sensory organs travels first to nerve cell bodies in the thalamus, where the signals are sorted and sent to the receiving areas on the cortex. The one exception is the olfactory system, which sends its stimuli directly to the cortex.

Below the thalamus is the thumbnail-sized hypothalamus. (*Hypo* means below. The term *hypothalamus* tells us this organ is below the thalamus.) It is a critical part of the autonomic system and, along with the pituitary gland, it controls functions necessary for homeostasis, maintaining the normal state of the body. For example, when the body gets too hot, the hypothalamus increases the perspiration rate. When the body temperature falls below normal, the rate of heat loss is slowed by contraction of the capillaries and shivering ensues, which produces a small amount of heat. The hypothalamus is the control center for the stimuli that underlie eating and drinking, as well. For example, if you have too much salt in your blood, the hypothalamus signals you to drink water to dilute the concentration of salt; if there is too much sugar in your blood, it suppresses your appetite. The hypothalamus also plays a role in regulating sex drive, sleep, aggressive behavior, and pleasure (Binney & Janson, 1990).

The hypothalamus plays an additional role, one that is essential for survival. If you've ever been frightened by a snake or a spider (or anything else, for that matter) and found your normal body state changing rapidly, heart beat increasing, palms getting sweaty, and respiration increasing, your hypothalamus is at work. It is this organ that controls the body's fight-or-flight response. We'll look more at this response and how it affects learning in Chapter 5.

Amygdala

Another brain structure highly involved in the fight-or-flight response, and located near the thalamus and hypothalamus, is the *amygdala*. If the brain could be said to have an alarm system, it would be these two almond-shaped structures (amygdala is the Greek word for almond) deep in the center of the brain. (It is also known as the amygdaloid complex because it is composed of three subdivisions, each connected to different brain structures or pathways.) The amygdala could be called the psychological sentinel of the brain, because it plays a major role in the control of emotion.

The amygdala could be called the psychological sentinel of the brain because it plays a major role in the control of emotion.

Various groups of cells in the amygdala are designed for different roles. One group links to the olfactory bulb and another to the cortex, especially the sensory association areas. Still another group links the amygdala to the brainstem and the hypothalamus. All incoming sensory data, except smell, travel first to the thalamus, which relays the information to the appropriate sensory-processing areas of the cortex. At the same time that the thalamus is sending information to the cortex, it sends the same information to the amygdala for evaluation. If the amygdala determines that the stimuli are potentially harmful, it triggers the hypothalamus, which in turn sends hormonal messages to the body, thus creating the physical changes that ready the body for action: heightened blood pressure, increased heart rate, and muscle contractions.

How does the amygdala "know" that a particular stimulus signals danger? There appear to be two sources of this "knowledge." One way the amygdala assesses the emotional relevance of

Once an episode is fully encoded in long-term memory, it apparently can be retrieved without the aid of the hippocampus.

a stimulus is by checking with the hippocampus, the structure that allows one to store conscious memories. (See the next section for more detailed information on the hippocampus.) If, for example, the particular stimulus is a curved shape, the amygdala, in checking with the hippocampus, may receive a message back that the curved shape looks like a snake and that snakes are potentially dangerous. This lets the amygdala know that it had better trigger the physiological processes necessary to keep you from being bitten.

However, the hippocampus does not seem to be responsible for all memory acquisition. Research on conditioned fear in animals has led to the broader hypothesis that the amygdala lays down unconscious memories in much the same way that the hippocampus lays down conscious ones (LeDoux, 1996). This suggests that the amygdala forms emotional memories that can trigger responses without the corresponding conscious recollections that tie the responses to a particular event. This may be the source of panic attacks and seemingly unreasonable phobias (Carter, 1998).

Hippocampus

Although its name is derived from the Latin word for sea-horse, the hippocampus looks more like two paws curving toward each other. Without it, you would not be able to remember where you parked your car, or anything else in your immediate past, as soon as you stopped giving it your attention. The hippocampus not only holds memory of your immediate past but also is the organ that eventually dispatches the memory to the cortex, where it is stored in what is called long-term memory.

According to Joseph LeDoux, professor at New York University and author of *The Emotional Brain*, the hippocampus appears to be crucial for you to be able to remember events in your immediate past, maybe even for a few years. Gradually over years, the hippocampus relinquishes its control over the memory to the cortex, where the memory appears to remain, perhaps for a lifetime, in long-term memory (LeDoux, 1996). In other words, once an episode is fully encoded in long-term memory, the hippocampus apparently is no longer needed for it to be retrieved. People who have suffered serious damage to the hippocampus cannot recall anything in their immediate past. Neither can they encode any new memories. An example of this deficit is vividly described in a famous case study of a man known as H. M. (Hilt, 1995).

In 1953, when H. M. was 27 years old, doctors performed radical surgery on his brain in an attempt to end the convulsive epileptic attacks he had been having since he was 16. The physicians removed large regions of the temporal lobes—brain tissue containing the major sites of his disease. Medically, the surgery was successful. H. M.'s seizures could now be controlled with medication. Because the hippocampus was included in the tissue that was removed, however, H. M. essentially lost his ability to form conscious, long-term memories of episodes or factual information. (These types of memory are called *episodic memory* and *declarative memory*. They stand in contrast to procedural memory, which does not require conscious recall. We'll look more closely at the various forms of memory in Chapter 7.) H. M. is an old man today, and he still lives to a degree in 1953, the year of his surgery. He can remember events that occurred up to about two years before his surgery, but he has no memory of the events of the past 45 years. Brenda Milner (see Hilt, 1995), at the Montreal Neurological Institute, has worked with H. M. extensively during this period, yet he has little idea of who she is.

Interestingly, H. M. is able to learn new motor-driven skills such as mirror writing or puzzle solving, but he does not remember learning them. (These are examples of procedural memory, which does not require processing in the hippocampus.)

Synapse Strengtheners

1. Select one of the major structures of the brain (such as the hippocampus) and, without looking back at the material, write a brief summary of where it is in the brain and what it does. Then go back and reread the information and see how well you recalled it.

2. Suppose, after reading this chapter, you are talking to a fellow educator who wants to know why one should know the names of the structures in the brain and what they do. What would you say to that person?

3. If you are reading this book as part of a study group, ask each member to select one or two major structures in the brain and prepare a presentation for the rest of the group on the location and function of these structures.

4. Plan one or more lessons to teach your students the parts of their brains.

Brain Anatomy—A Short Course: The Cortex

3

Thus far, all the structures we have been discussing operate at an unconscious level. Michael Gazzaniga, Director of the Center for Cognitive Neuroscience at Dartmouth College, emphasizes that most mental processes controlling and contributing to our conscious experience occur *outside* our conscious awareness (Gazzaniga, Ivry, & Mangun, 1998). We are consciously aware of only a small part of what is going on inside our brain. Such structures as the brainstem, cerebellum, amygdala, and hippocampus play critical roles in our ability to process information and form memories (and eventually to become aware of them), but we are not *consciously* aware of the activities of these structures. We now turn our attention to the part of the brain that allows us to be aware, to recognize, and to talk about how we're feeling and what we're thinking—the structures that operate at the conscious level.

We are consciously aware of only a small part of what is going on inside our brain.

The Cerebral Cortex

Covering the cerebrum (the Latin word for brain) is a thin layer known as the cerebral cortex, or neocortex. The word *cortex* is derived from the Latin word for bark; to a degree, the cortex resembles the bark of a tree. It is wrinkled, is about 1/32- to 1/4-

inch thick, and is the so-called "grey matter" of the brain. The cerebral cortex is made up of six layers of cells, their dendrites, and some axons. If the cerebral cortex were taken off the brain and stretched flat, it would be about the size of a pillow case or the page of a newspaper. Studies of human brains by neurosurgeons, neurologists, and neuroscientists have shown that different areas (lobes) of the cerebral cortex have separate functions. Let's look at the four main lobes, which take their names from the skull bones they underlie, and at their major roles in processing information.

Occipital Lobes

Located at the lower central back of the brain are the occipital lobes, the primary brain centers for processing visual stimuli. (See Figure 3.1.) Covered by cortical tissue, this area of the brain is also called the visual cortex. It is split into many subdivisions, each playing a role in processing visual data coming into the brain from the outside world. (Recall that visual stimuli are first relayed through the thalamus.) When stimuli reach the visual cortex, they are first processed in the primary visual perception area, where millions of neurons are further organized into areas designed to process different aspects of vision. Through intensive work in mapping the visual cortex, scientists have discovered motion-sensitive cells, color-sensitive cells, and straight-line cells. There are also areas for general scanning, stereo vision, depth, distance, and object detection (Carter, 1998). Michael Gazzaniga, in the book *Cognitive Neuroscience*, reports that between 30 and 35 of these visual areas have been identified in the occipital lobes of monkeys (Gazzaniga et al., 1998).

Once the incoming information has been assembled in these areas (has been perceived), it then travels to the secondary, or visual association, area, which compares the information with

If the cortex were taken off the brain and stretched flat, it would be about the size of a pillow case or the page of a newspaper.

what you've seen before and lets you know whether you are seeing an orange or a tree.

Note that two people can look at the same thing and focus
on something different, or "see" different things. What you
attend to visually is the coordinated functioning of several brain
systems. First, the visual perception area allows perception of the
actual object. Your visual cortex then communicates with other
brain systems to determine what visual information you have

~ Figure 3.1 ~
THE OCCIPITAL LOBES

stored previously. Visual stimuli do not become meaningful until the sensory perceptions are matched with previously stored cognitive associations. In addition, we often prime our brains to pay attention to certain stimuli over others, such as looking for a friend in a crowd of people or, when directed by the teacher, to see a shape of a certain color among a large number of different-colored shapes. This is why telling students the objective of an activity is usually desirable. It allows the brain to anticipate the critical features or ideas and increase the likelihood that the brain will focus on the essential information.

Two people can look at the same thing and focus on something different, or "see" different things.

Temporal Lobes

On either side of the brain, just above the ears, are two lobes that curve forward from the occipital lobes to below the frontal lobes. These are the temporal lobes, whose main function is to process auditory stimuli. (See Figure 3.2.) The temporal lobes are composed of several subdivisions that cope with hearing, language, and some aspects of memory, especially auditory memory. Hearing is often considered the most important sense for humans. It allows us to communicate with each another and gives us information vital for our survival: The sound of an oncoming train tells us to move away from the track, or the sound of steps behind us tells us to check and see if we know who or what is making the sound. Deafness can be more debilitating than blindness, even though humans are highly visual creatures.

Like the occipital lobes, the temporal lobes have many subdivisions. When the primary auditory region of the temporal lobes is stimulated, sensations of sound are produced. In addition, an auditory association area has links to the primary region and other parts of the brain and aids in the perception of auditory inputs, allowing us to recognize what we are hearing. Within these two major regions, groups of neurons have specific jobs, such as registering a sound's loudness, pitch, or timbre.

At the conjunction of the left occipital, parietal, and temporal lobes (but lying mostly in the temporal lobe) is a group of cells known as Wernicke's Area. This area is critical for speech. Wernicke's Area—located in the left hemisphere—allows us to comprehend or interpret speech and to put words together in correct syntax when speaking. We'll see a little later that another area (Broca's Area) is necessary to produce speech.

~ Figure 3.2 ~
THE TEMPORAL LOBES

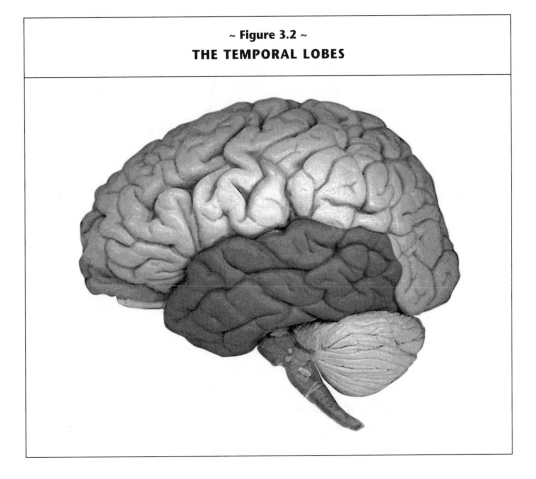

Parietal Lobes

Sometimes, as the result of a stroke in the right hemisphere of the brain, persons are left with a strange disorder called anosognosia, meaning "lack of knowledge of illness." These people are often paralyzed on the left side of their bodies, but are unaware of their problem. They treat the left side of their bodies as if it wasn't there, refusing to comb their hair on that side or even refusing to put clothes on that half of the body. To understand how this strange disorder could occur, we need to look at the part of the cortex that handles spatial awareness and orientation.

At the top of the brain is a flat, plate-like area in each hemisphere called the parietal lobes. (See Figure 3.3.) These lobes consist of two major subdivisions—the anterior and posterior parts—that play different, but complementary, roles.

Within the anterior (front) part of the parietal lobes, immediately behind the motor cortex, lies a strip of cells called the somatosensory cortex. (See Figure 3.4.) Just as we need to send information to the muscles in our body about when and how to move, we also need to be able to receive information, such as touch and temperature from our environment; sensations of pain and pressure from the skin; and the positions of our limbs (proprioception). This is accomplished by the somatosensory cortex, the primary region responsible for receiving incoming sensory stimuli. Each part of the body is represented by a specific area on the surface of the somatosensory cortex. The more sensitive a part of the body, the greater the area needed to interpret its messages. For example, the lips, tongue, and throat have the largest number of receptors. Damage to this part of a parietal lobe interferes with the perception of touch and pain and with the knowledge of the body's position in space.

The posterior (rear) part of the parietal lobes continuously analyzes and integrates all this information to give you a sense of spatial awareness. The brain must know at all times where each part of the body is located and its relation to its surroundings. Damage to this part of the parietal lobes often results in clumsiness in manipulating objects (apraxia).

A final role of the parietal lobes is in maintaining focus or spatial attention. When one is focused on a particular stimulus, or when attention shifts from location to location, activation of

~ Figure 3.3 ~
THE PARIETAL LOBES

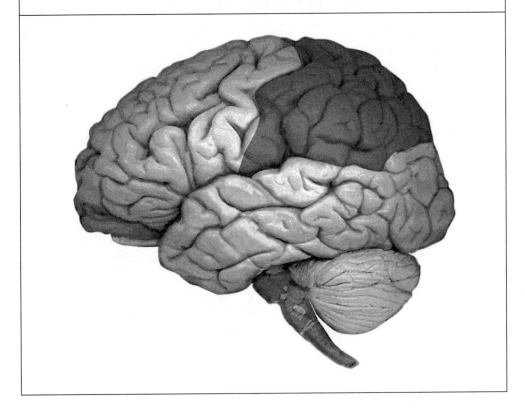

the parietal lobes can be seen through brain-imaging techniques. As a stimulus becomes less meaningful, however, the attention wanes. For example, if you are wearing shoes that are tight or painful, your focus will be maintained on your feet. But if you take off the tight shoes, the sensory receptors stop sending so much information and your attention shifts to something else.

Frontal Lobes

The frontal lobes occupy the largest part of the cortex (28 percent) and perform the most complex functions. (See Figure 3.5.)

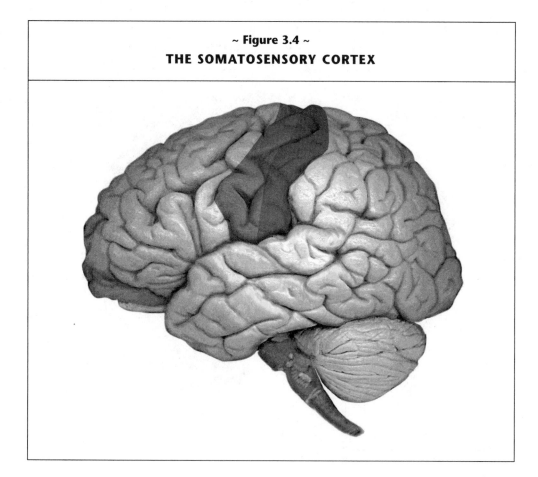

~ Figure 3.4 ~
THE SOMATOSENSORY CORTEX

Located in the front of the brain and extending back to the top of the head, the frontal lobe has expanded rapidly over the past 20,000 generations and is what most clearly distinguishes us from our forefathers. Your abilities to move parts of your body at will, think about the past, plan for the future, focus your attention, reflect, make decisions, solve problems, and engage in conversation are all possible because of this highly developed area of your brain. But perhaps more amazing than any of these functions is the fact that the frontal lobes of the cerebral cortex are what allow you to be consciously aware of all these thoughts and actions.

The frontal lobes of the cerebral cortex allow us to be consciously aware of all these actions.

~ **Figure 3.5** ~
THE FRONTAL LOBES

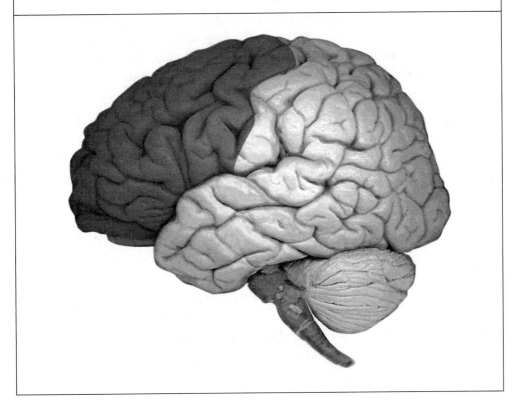

The functions of the frontal lobes fall into two main categories: sensorimotor processing and cognition. Toward the back of the frontal lobes is a strip of cells that stretches across the top of the brain, forming a sort of band along a path just in front of the ears like the connecting piece in earphones. This strip is known as the motor cortex. (See Figure 3.6.) Nearly all neural activity directing muscular movement originates in the brain's motor cortex. Different areas of this strip govern the movements of specific muscles in the body. Similar to the somatosensory cortex, every part of your body, from your toes up to your lips, has a corresponding region in the motor cortex, but all parts of the body are not equally represented.

Nearly all neural activity directing muscular movement originates in the brain's motor cortex.

Certain muscles must carry out much more precise, fine-motor movements than others, so the areas of the motor cortex controlling these muscles are disproportionately large. For example, the areas governing the fingers, lips, and tongue are much larger than the area governing the small of the back, because the small of the back doesn't have to carry out precise motions.

Just in front of the motor cortex is a supplemental motor area. This area contains an extremely important group of nerve cells known as Broca's Area. This is the part of the cortex that allows you to speak. Broca's Area is located in the left hemisphere of the supplemental motor area in about 95 percent of the population. (The other 5 per cent, approximately 30 per cent of left-handed persons, have the speech production area in the right hemisphere.) It probably is not surprising to find that Broca's Area is connected to Wernicke's Area in the temporal lobes by a bundle of nerve fibers. This linkage is important because, before any speech can be uttered, its form and the appropriate words must first be assembled in Wernicke's Area and then relayed to Broca's Area to be translated into the proper sounds. This information is then passed to the motor cortex for vocal production (Ackerman, 1992).

The large part of the frontal lobes situated in front of the secondary motor zones has sometimes been called the "silent" area, meaning it is free from processing sensory data and governing movement. Called the prefrontal cortex, it is proportionately much larger in humans than in other species. This may be the part of our brains that most clearly defines what it means to be human, the part that separates us from animals. As Sandra Ackerman, in her book *Discovering the Brain*, states:

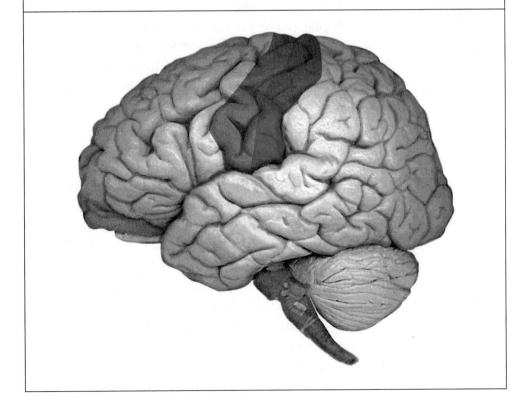

~ **Figure 3.6** ~
THE MOTOR CORTEX

Humans have the least stereotyped, most flexible lifestyle of all animal species, and it is believed that the cortex must in some way be related to liberating the individual from the fixed, pre-determined patterns of behavior (Ackerman, 1992, p. 15).

The prefrontal cortex is sometimes called the association cortex. It is here that information is synthesized from both the inner and outer sensory worlds, that associations between objects and their names are made, and that the highest forms of mental activities take place. Our human cortex allows us to build cathedrals, compose symphonies, dream and plan for a better future, love, hate, and experience emotional pain, because it is in the cortex that consciousness—our ability to be aware of what we are thinking, feeling, and doing—emerges.

Recent findings have implicated a part of the prefrontal cortex as critical for emotional self-regulation (Siegel, 1999). The orbitofrontal cortex (so named because of its proximity to the eye socket, or orbit) appears to have the responsibility for evaluating and regulating the emotional impulses emanating from the lower centers of the brain. This new finding regarding the orbitofrontal cortex deserves our attention and study. It may eventually help us understand everyday failures of self-regulation, such as road rage in adults or temper tantrums in children. It is possible that these inappropriate responses are the result of an injury to the brain, causing a sort of short-circuiting of the wiring of the orbitofrontal cortex; genetic predisposition also may be a contributing factor. Some researchers believe, however, that the most common determiner of failure to self-regulate emotional responses is the lack of emotionally consistent parenting in the early years (Siegel, 2000).

Many parts of the brain must work together in a complex set of interactions for us to engage in a seemingly simple act. For example, Broca's Area, Wernicke's Area, and the motor cortex all must work together for us to speak a sentence. The same is true of

Our human cortex allows us to build cathedrals, compose symphonies, dream and plan for a better future, love, hate, and experience emotional pain because it is in the cortex that consciousness—our ability to be aware of what we are thinking, feeling, and doing—emerges.

walking across a room, lifting a glass, or recognizing a friend. Although the structure and function of the major structures of the brain have been addressed separately here, it is extremely important to remember that no structure works alone in this complex system.

Are We of Two Minds?

Throughout this chapter and the previous one, we noted that the various structures of the brain come in pairs. (The exception is the single pineal gland, which led Socrates to designate it the seat of the soul.) Looking down from the top, the whole brain appears to be composed of two seemingly identical halves. A deep groove known as the longitudinal fissure runs the length of the brain and travels nearly halfway down into its center, dividing the brain into two parts, resembling an enormous walnut.

The functions and roles of these two halves, known as the right and left hemispheres, have been debated for centuries. As early as 400 B.C., Hippocrates wrote about the possibility of the duality of the human brain. In 1874, Englishman John Hughlings Jackson introduced the idea of the brain having a "leading" hemisphere (Binney & Janson, 1990). In the 1970s and 1980s, and even today to a lesser degree, it was common to hear people referred to as right-brained or left-brained, generally signifying that they were predominantly verbal and analytical (left-brained) or artistic and emotional (right-brained). This idea of a rigid right/left divide spawned a small industry of books and courses (with topics such as drawing on the right side of the brain or developing a right-brained management style), all designed to encourage right-brained activity and thinking. Even educators attempted to direct more of their instruction to the right side of the brain. As sometimes happens with many new theories, we took a complex subject and, with good intentions, generated

Many parts of the brain must work together in a complex set of interactions for us to engage in a seemingly simple act.

applications that were far removed from the actual scientific research. (Scientists have even coined a name for the unbridled enthusiasm for our "two brains." They call it "dichotomania.")

None of these theories and ideas about the roles of the hemispheres was totally inaccurate, or totally accurate. Over the past two decades, a large body of research has emerged on the roles of the cerebral hemispheres. As often happens, the more we study any part of the brain, the more we learn just how complex it is; our hemispheres are no exception. New findings have caused some of the major researchers and writers in this field to modify their earlier views. Which of the older views still hold true, and what new information do we have about the hemispheres and their functions?

It has long been known that, for the most part, the left hemisphere of the brain governs the right side of the body and the right hemisphere, the left. We've also known that the two hemispheres are joined by several bundles of fibers known as commissures. The largest of these is a four-inch-long bundle of fibers known as the corpus callosum. The corpus callosum is the largest fiber system in the brain. It is composed of about 300 million axons, the appendages of neurons that are responsible for sending messages to other cells.

This much information has been around for a long time, but the realization that each hemisphere has specialties is relatively new. In the early 1960s, several neuroscientists at the California Institute of Technology were looking for ways to control epileptic seizures. Epileptic seizures, or electrical disturbances, in one hemisphere often cross over the corpus callosum and trigger a seizure in the other hemisphere. Roger Sperry, a neuroscience researcher, along with neurosurgeons Joseph Bogen and Philip Vogel, speculated that cutting through the corpus callosum might prevent the electrical activity from crossing between hemispheres and thus stop or minimize the seizures (Ornstein, 1997). They guessed

Scientists have coined a name for the unbridled enthusiasm for our "two brains." They call it "dichotomania."

right. After the surgery to sever the corpus callosum, the patients' symptoms diminished considerably and the patients appeared to function perfectly well in their daily activities. But studies on these "split-brain" patients revealed that something unusual had happened. If the patients held an object (such as a pencil) hidden from sight in their right hands, they could name and describe it. But when the pencil was held in the left hand out of sight, they claimed they held nothing. This finding was puzzling and led to further studies on these split-brain patients. Much of this research was conducted by Roger Sperry and his colleagues, Michael Gazzaniga and Joseph Bogen; and it led to an understanding that the two hemispheres are indeed specialized in what they do (Gazzaniga, Bogen, & Sperry, 1962). From this research, we now believe that the reason split-brained patients could not name the pencil when it was held out of sight in the left hand is that the left hand communicates largely with the right hemisphere. This hemisphere is limited in its ability to produce speech. Therefore when the corpus callosum is severed, and the hemispheres can't communicate with one another, the "silent" right hemisphere doesn't allow the person to name the object. (Recall that for approximately 95 percent of the population, the left hemisphere is dominant for language and speech, while the roles are reversed in some left-handers.)

Further research revealed other specializations of the hemispheres, as well. Melodies are perceived better in the left ear/right hemisphere than in the right ear/left hemisphere. Emotions appear to be lateralized, as well, with the right hemisphere processing the more negative emotions and the left more positive and optimistic ones (Ornstein, 1997). Persons with left-hemisphere damage have difficulty recognizing faces, while damage to the right hemisphere often causes people to have difficulty finding their way around.

Probably one of the most critical aspects of hemispheric specialization is the issue of context.

Probably one of the most critical aspects of hemispheric specialization is the issue of context. Our understanding of what we read or our comprehension of what we hear depends on the context within which it occurs. For example, the comment, "Oh, that's wonderful!" can be expressed with joy or with sarcasm. Unless you can compute the context through body language, the intonation of the person speaking, or the sentence that preceded it in the narrative, the sentence is virtually meaningless. Interestingly, it is the right hemisphere that decodes the external information, allowing us to create an overall understanding of what is said or what we read. The right hemisphere allows us to "get" the joke or to respond appropriately to a comment. This is the hemisphere that assembles the whole field of view, allowing us to see the forest as well as the individual trees. The right hemisphere gives us an overall view of the world (Ornstein, 1997).

The research on split-brain patients is interesting, but what about the vast majority of us who have an intact corpus callosum? Are our hemispheres lateralized in the same way? Researcher Robert Ornstein has done extensive studies of normal people using EEGs that validate the findings generated by studying the split-brain patients. Ornstein and his colleagues asked people to perform simple tasks, such as writing a letter to a friend (left hemisphere) or arranging blocks into a pattern (right hemisphere), and recorded their brain waves as they worked. The researchers compared alpha waves (indicating an awake brain on idle) and beta waves (an awake brain actively processing information) during these two activities. When writing a letter, the left hemisphere showed more beta activity and the right more alpha. The opposite was true when the person was arranging blocks. Ornstein characterizes this phenomenon as a "turning on" of the hemisphere primarily responsible for a particular action, while the other hemisphere temporarily turns off (Ornstein, 1997).

Although it now seems clear that our hemispheres each have their specialities, we must remember that they work in concert at all times. In your brain right now, the information arriving in one hemisphere is immediately available to the other side. The responses of the two hemispheres are so closely coordinated that they produce a single view of the world, not two. For example, when you are engaged in conversation, it is your left hemisphere that allows you to produce speech, but it is your right hemisphere that gives the intonation to your speech. This, in turn, allows your listeners to use their right hemispheres to judge the context and fully comprehend the intended meaning of your words. The specializations of each hemisphere develop to their fullest when informed by the opposite hemisphere. The two halves of your brain work together in a beautifully coordinated partnership. This collaboration is described by Robert Ornstein (1997) in his book, *The Right Mind*:

> They are in the same body, after all, even though they're a couple of inches apart. They have the same cerebellum, the same brainstem, the same spinal cord. Each half of the human brain shares years of experiences with the other. They eat the same cereal in the morning and the same burger at lunch (and thus receive the same changes in their blood supply); they share the same hormones. Identical neurotransmitter cocktails mainline through each of them, they listen to the same nonsense from other people, they look at the same TV programs, and they go to the same parties. And neither hemisphere operates anything on its own, any more than we walk with one foot or the other, or whether the area of a rectangle is dependent on its length or width. *Almost nothing is regulated solely by the left or right hemisphere* (Ornstein, 1997, p. 68).

Although it now seems clear that our hemispheres each have their specialities, we must remember that they work in concert at all times.

Teaching to Both Halves of the Brain

Does knowing the special contributions of each hemisphere to information processing mean much to us as educators? Does it help to know that the left hemisphere processes the text, and the right provides the context? Maybe there are important implications that go beyond the "teaching to the right side of the brain" activities we've all heard about and perhaps tried in our classrooms. Perhaps we need to put more emphasis on teaching to *both* halves of the brain, since they work together all the time. Content (the text in which the left hemisphere excels) is important, but text without context (the speciality of the right hemisphere) is often meaningless. We need to teach content within a context that is meaningful to students, and that connects to their own lives and experiences. This is teaching to both halves of the brain. Too often, the curriculum is taught in isolation, with little effort put into helping students see how the information is, or could be, used in their lives. Too many students never comprehend the "big picture" of how the content they are learning fits in the larger scheme of things.

How many of you made good grades in certain subjects and have to admit that you've never used what you learned because it was taught out of context? Does what you learned in history help you understand events occurring in the world today? Does the A you earned in algebra assist you in solving problems in your everyday life? If we don't connect the curriculum to the learner's experience, much of the information gets lost, and we waste time having students engage in meaningless memorization rituals. According to David Perkins, we produce students with "fragile knowledge" that they either don't remember after the test or don't know when or how to use (Perkins, 1992). Perhaps an increased understanding of the cerebral hemispheres will assist us in designing curriculum and pedagogy that results not only in

The more we understand the brain, the better we'll be able to design instruction to match how it learns best.

increased student understanding of information taught, but also in increased ability to use the information appropriately.

The information contained in Chapters 2 and 3 is meant to serve as a reference for the rest of the book. When various neural structures are mentioned, you can refer back to these pages to refresh your memory, thereby strengthening the neural connections that were made when you first read the information. In the next chapter, we'll look at how these neural connections are formed and the role of these connections in memory and learning.

Synapse Strengtheners

1. Without looking at the book, make a rough sketch of the brain and label the four lobes. Under each label, list the major functions of that lobe.

2. Explain to a friend why the terms "right-brained" and "left-brained" do not accurately explain the functions of the cerebral hemispheres.

3. If you are meeting with colleagues in a study group, devote a session to a discussion of how to teach to both halves of the brain simultaneously.

4 | How Neurons Communicate

All human behavior can be traced to the communication among neurons. Every thought you think, every emotion you feel, every movement you make, your awareness of the world around you, and your ability to read these words are possible because neurons "talk" to each other. How do these cells accomplish such a variety of tasks? What does the communication look like? We once believed that transmission between neurons was simply an electrical current flowing from one neuron to the next. Today we know that this is true for only a few of the neurons in the nervous system. Our focus will be on the majority of neurons in the mature human brain, which do not communicate solely using electricity.

The Action Potential: The Brain's Electrical Signal

Most neurons communicate with each other by means of both electrical and chemical signals. We have known for many years that the brain produces some type of electricity. As early as 1875, English physiologist Richard Caton recorded weak electrical currents in the brains of monkeys. It wasn't until 1929, however, that German psychiatrist Hans Berger first recorded electrical signals in the human brain (Greenfield, 1997). Today, the currents generated by the billions of neurons in the brain are commonly measured using the electroencephalogram (EEG). What is the source of these electrical signals? How do they compare with the electricity we use to operate our computers and our appliances?

Nerve impulses that travel along the axons in neurons are bioelectrical currents and not the mechanical electrical currents that flow through the wiring in our homes. In our brains, these impulses are the result of the movement of four common ions: sodium, potassium, calcium, and chloride. (Ions are atoms that have either a positive or a negative electrical charge. Positive ions, like the sodium, potassium, and calcium ions, are atoms that have lost one or more electrons. Negative ions, like the chloride ion, are atoms that have gained one or more electrons.) Specific channels in the neuron cell membrane allow ions to move from one side of the membrane to the other. Potassium ions are distributed inside the membrane of a neuron at rest; sodium, calcium, and chloride ions are distributed along the outside of the normally more or less impermeable membrane. The inside of the neuron has a slight excess of negatively charged ions with respect to the outside. The difference, called the *resting potential*, is usually expressed as a negative value, about –70-thousandths of a volt. In other words, a neuron at rest holds a slight negative charge.

When nothing much is happening, a neuron usually sends impulses down the axon at a relatively slow, irregular rate. When a neuron is stimulated (receives excitatory signals from another neuron), however, the sodium channels in the membrane open and the positively charged sodium ions enter the cell. This makes the potential difference temporarily more positive inside than outside. As soon as this occurs, however, positively charged potassium ions leave the cell, changing the voltage to more negative than normal. This brief change in the potential difference usually lasts for about one millisecond and is known as an action potential. The action potential spreads down the axon as the sodium channels open sequentially, somewhat like falling dominoes (Restak, 1994). Each axon channel opens up the next channel, just as each domino in a line has to knock over only the next. The chain reaction that results is a great energy saver compared to physically pushing over 50 dominoes one by one. This impulse moves only in one direction until it reaches the end of the axon. Though all action potentials have the same intensity, the strength of the message can vary, depending on how frequently the action potential is generated. Some neurons can fire up to 500 action potentials a second. The more normal rates, however, are 30 to 100 potentials a second. The speed of an action potential varies according to the diameter of the axon and whether or not it is insulated with myelin. Action potentials travel at speeds up to 220 miles per hour. This speed is much slower than that of a computer, but is fast by biological criteria (Greenfield, 1997).

Now that we have taken a look at the electrical component of neural transmission, we are in a better position to understand the chemical component.

The Brain's Own Pharmacy: The Chemical Signals

During the night of Easter Sunday, 1921, Austrian physiologist Otto Loewi had a dream. He awoke, jotted down some notes, and went back to sleep. In the morning he could not decipher his notes, but he knew that he had written down something important. The next night he had the same dream and immediately got up and went to his laboratory to perform the experiment suggested by his dream. It was designed around two frog hearts, which were being kept alive in special oxygenated chambers filled with a fluid similar to that normally found in the body. It was already

Action potentials travel at speeds up to about 220 miles per hour!

known that if the vagus nerve (which enervates the heart) is stimulated, the heart slows down. Loewi stimulated the vagus nerve of one of the hearts, then transferred the fluid that had surrounded it to the second heart. Even though the second heart had not been stimulated, it too slowed down. Loewi concluded that there must have been some chemical released into the fluid when the first heart was stimulated, and when that fluid was applied to the second heart, the effects were the same as on the first heart. He called this chemical *vagusstoff*, which was identified in 1933 as the transmitter acetylcholine. The discovery of the effect of acetylcholine on the heart was to have profound implications for understanding how neurons communicate with each other (Bear, Conners, & Paradiso, 1996).

Acetylcholine is one of the brain's own chemical messengers, which are generally called neurotransmitters. Many neurotransmitters today are fairly well known. You've probably heard of dopamine, serotonin, and the endorphins. Many more exist, however—perhaps as many as 100. Some of these neurotransmitters are generated within the cell bodies of neurons, and others are synthesized within the axon terminals. Regardless of their source, all the neurotransmitter molecules are eventually stored in small sacs, or vesicles, in the bulb-like terminals of the axon branches, where they will be ready to go to work when needed.

Neurotransmitters are generally either excitatory or inhibitory, meaning that they either increase or decrease the probability that a neuron will fire. At first glance it might be difficult to see why there would be times when you would want neural activity inhibited. But imagine what it would be like if all the neurons in your motor cortex, or any other part of your brain for that matter, were firing all the time. Neurotransmitters are fascinating chemicals, and we'll take a closer look at them a little later in this chapter.

Imagine what it would be like if all the neurons in your motor cortex, or any other part of your brain for that matter, were firing all the time!

The Synapse

The next step in understanding neural communication is to look at how the electrical and chemical components come together to allow information to be passed from cell to cell within the central nervous system. This all-important action takes place at the junction of the axon terminal of one neuron and a dendrite on the cell body of a second neuron. This junction is known as a synapse. (See Figure 4.1.) The axon terminal and the

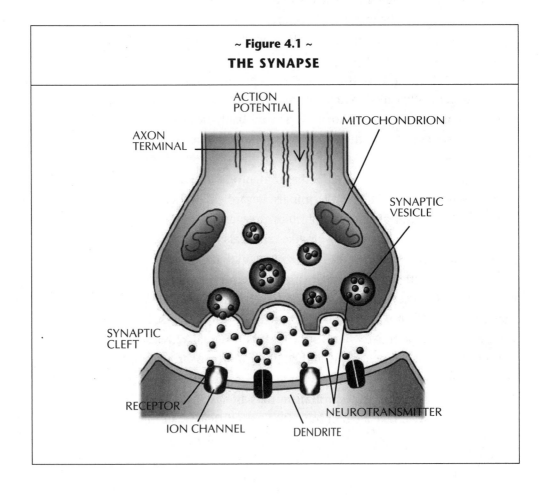

~ Figure 4.1 ~
THE SYNAPSE

membrane of the dendrite are separated by an infinitesimal gap called the synaptic cleft. Most synapses take place on the spines of the dendrites, but 15 to 20 percent of the synapses occur on the cell body itself.

When the action potential reaches the terminal of an axon, it stimulates the opening of some of the vesicles and thus triggers the release of one or more neurotransmitters into the synaptic cleft. The neurotransmitter molecules diffuse across the cleft. The more action potentials that arrive at the terminal, the more molecules are released into the gap. The electrical signal of the action potential has now been converted into a chemical signal, and the synaptic cleft is crossed within thousandths of a second. (At one point scientists believed that each neuron produced only one neurotransmitter. We now know that a neuron may release two or more transmitters at a single synapse; it may even switch transmitters.)

Once the neurotransmitter molecules reach the other side of the synapse, each molecule makes contact with its target, the postsynaptic or receiving neuron. How is the contact made? On the dendrite of the receiving neuron are special large protein molecules that are called receptors. Each neurotransmitter has a different shape, and the receptors are specifically designed for the shape of the neurotransmitter they are receiving, as precisely as a key is made for a lock. The neurotransmitter molecule fits into the receptor site, opening or closing ion channels on the membrane of the target neuron. Just as a change in the potential difference of the axon membrane generated an action potential, a change in the potential difference in the membrane of the dendrite causes the stimulation of the target neuron (Restak,1994).

This change then becomes one of the many electrical signals that will be conducted down the dendrites to the cell body of the postsynaptic neuron. The dendrites have now converted the chemical signal back into an electrical signal, thus, in a sense,

Each neurotransmitter has a different shape, and the receptors are specifically designed for the shape of the neurotransmitter they are receiving, as precisely as a key is made for a lock.

completing the cycle. Because a neuron can have thousands of dendrites, and the dendrites are covered with tiny spines that effectively increase the surface area, this process is occurring at thousands of sites. As soon as the electrical signals from all the involved dendrites arrive at the cell body, the neuron adds up all inputs to determine whether to generate an action potential. It is somewhat like a conscientious member of Congress who tallies the wishes of all her constituents before deciding how to vote. If the net change in voltage is sufficiently large, the ion channels will open near the cell body, the neuron will generate an action potential, and the "impulse" will begin its travel down the axon. If the voltage isn't high enough, the cell will not generate an electrical impulse, and the neuron will not fire. Remember that the neurotransmitters (being either excitatory or inhibitory) determine whether the net change in voltage is large enough to generate an action potential (Crick, 1994; Restak, 1994; Thompson, 1985).

During this electrochemical process, the neurotransmitter involved is not "used up" in the receptor. Once the neurotransmitter has accomplished its task, it is rapidly cleared from the synapse. This can happen in three ways:

1. Through reuptake channels, the axon terminal of the cell reabsorbs many neurotransmitter molecules; the axon then "recycles" them to be used again.

2. The enzymes present in the synaptic cleft destroy some neurotransmitter molecules.

3. Still other molecules diffuse out of the cleft and are carried away as waste material by the cerebrospinal fluid.

More About Neurotransmitters

In his book *Receptors*, Restak explains that no matter at what level we study the brain, whether behavioral, microscopic, or

Restak suggests that all things mental, both normal functions and disorders of thought, originate from some corresponding order or disorder in chemical processes.

molecular, chemical messengers (and their receptors) underpin all behavior. Thoughts and emotions are the results of chemical processes in the brain, and so are the twitches of muscles. Restak suggests that all things mental, both normal functions and disorders of thought, originate from some corresponding order or disorder in chemical processes (Restak, 1994). A basic awareness of how these chemical transmitters work is essential not only for understanding memory and learning, but also for understanding the effects of drugs, medications, and foods on the brain.*

Types of Neurotransmitters

Our bodies often put common and familiar things to new uses. This is certainly true of neurotransmitters. Amino acids are the building blocks of proteins and are essential to life. With the exception of acetylcholine, all neurotransmitters are (1) amino acids, (2) derived from amino acids (amines), or (3) constructed of amino acids (peptides). Figure 4.2 shows some representatives of these three types.

Amino Acids

Amino acids are derived from protein foods and are found throughout the brain and the body. In the brain they are involved in rapid point-to-point communication between neurons. Of the 20 common amino acids, four function as neurotransmitters: glycine, gamma-amino butyric acid (GABA), aspartate, and glutamate.

---

*To be classified as a neurotransmitter, a chemical compound in the brain must meet a half-dozen criteria. It must (1) be created in the neuron, (2) be stored in the neuron, (3) be released by the neuron in sufficient quantity to bring about some physical effect, (4) demonstrate the same effect experimentally that it does in living tissue, and (6) have means for shutting off its effect (Ackerman, 1992).

Brain
Matters: Translating Research into Classroom Practice

Glycine and GABA (which is made from glycine) always carry an inhibitory message. The cerebellum, retina, and spinal cord, as well as many other parts of the brain, all use GABA circuits to inhibit signals. Nearly one-third of synapses in the cortex are GABA synapses.

Glutamate and aspartate always carry an excitatory message at the synapse (Crick, 1994). Pathways that carry these excitatory amino acids are widely distributed throughout the brain. Without them, brain functioning would cease. Glutamate is used extensively by the hippocampus and is a critical neurotransmitter for memory and learning (Sapolsky, 1994).

Amines

Amines (also called monoamines) are chemically modified amino acids that act more slowly than other amino acids. Rather than acting directly at the synapse, they generally modulate the actions of the amino acid neurotransmitters and for this reason are often called neuromodulators. They bias how the target neu-

~ Figure 4.2 ~ TYPES OF NEUROTRANSMITTERS		
Amino Acids	**Amines**	**Peptides**
Glutamate	Epinephrine (or adrenalin)	Endorphins
Glycine	Norepinephrine (or noradrenalin)	Substance P
Aspartate	Dopamine	Vasopressin
GABA (gamma-aminobutyric acid)	Serotonin	Cortisol (glucocorticoid)
	Acetylcholine (not truly an amine, but often included)	

ron responds to an incoming message, even though they do not pass it along. Produced in the brain stem or other subcortical structures, they are dispersed throughout the brain by an intricate network of axons much as a sprinkler system dispersing water to all parts of the lawn. Amine neurotransmitters are found in much lower concentrations—one one-thousandth as much as GABA and glutamate. They may be lower in concentration, but as we will see, they are important to understand because of the powerful effects they have on many parts of the brain. Some of the most noteworthy of the amines are as follows.

Our body often has a way of using the same substances and structures in different ways.

Epinephrine. Our body often has a way of using the same substances and structures in different ways. A prime example is epinephrine, also known as adrenaline, which acts as both a hormone and a neurotransmitter. (Hormones are chemicals—peptides or proteins—that are produced in one part of the body and that, when released, tell another part of the body what to do. In other words, they act at a distance from their point of origin.) As a hormone, epinephrine is synthesized in the adrenal glands that sit on top of the kidneys. It is involved in the stress response, also known as the "fight-or-flight" response. When this system is activated, epinephrine acts to speed up the heart, restrict blood vessels, relax the tubules in the lungs, and generally put the entire body in a state of alert. Scientists have also found epinephrine in the brain, where it acts as a neurotransmitter. In this case, it acts not at a distance but extremely close to its point of origin. Its structure and function are similar to norepinephrine, which is next on our list.

Norepinephrine, also known as noradrenaline, is the primary neurotransmitter for the arousal mechanism of the fight-or-flight syndrome.

Norepinephrine. Norepinephrine, also known as noradrenaline, is the primary neurotransmitter for the arousal mechanism of the fight-or-flight syndrome. In this role, it is responsible for dilating the pupils of the eyes, strengthening and speeding the heartbeat, and inhibiting the processes of digestion. It also stimulates the adrenal glands to release epinephrine and the liver to release large amounts of glucose, making more energy available to the muscles.

Norepinephrine has a chemical composition and function similar to epinephrine. Like epinephrine, it serves more than one purpose in the body and the brain. Norepinephrine is produced in a small structure in the brain stem (the locus coeruleus) but has pathways that project to the hypothalamus, the cerebellum, and even to the frontal cortex. These projections allow the norepinephrine to control overall activity level and mood, such as increasing the level of wakefulness. Some preliminary studies have looked at the relationship between depression and norepinephrine. Though researchers have not yet found anything conclusive, there is a wide consensus that depression can be helped by two classes of drugs—one that blocks an enzyme that normally breaks down norepinephrine in the synaptic cleft, and another that slows its reuptake (Ackerman, 1992).

Dopamine. Dopamine is a neurotransmitter that plays several roles in brain functioning, but two of its major roles are to control conscious motor activity and to enhance pleasurable feelings in the brain's reward system. It is chemically similar to norepinephrine and is synthesized in several locations in the brain. Like most of the other amines, dopamine is conveyed to other parts of the brain by means of widespread pathways. Dopamine pathways lead to the frontal lobes as well as to the hypothalamus. The motor tremors and other effects of Parkinson's disease are caused when a group of cells in the brainstem (the substantia nigra) fails to produce sufficient dopamine for efficient motor functioning. Another site where dopamine is produced is in a cluster of cells deep within the middle of the brain called the ventral tegmental area (VTA). This area is known to be a mediating area for maternal behavior, as well as for addiction. Later in this chapter we'll look at how dopamine and other neurotransmitters are related to the reward system and to drug addiction.

Serotonin. Serotonin is, for the layperson, probably one of the best-known neurotransmitters. It has been called the "feel good" transmitter. Indeed, like dopamine and norepinephrine, it is a mood enhancer. Unlike these other amines, however, serotonin appears to affect mood by calming rather than stimulating the brain. Serotonin's notoriety is the result of its relation to depression, which affects millions of people. Antidepressants such as Prozac, Zoloft, and Paxil work by inhibiting the reuptake of serotonin at the synapse, thus increasing its effect. Serotonin is also involved in memory, sleep, control of appetite, and regulation of body temperature.

Serotonin is probably one of the neurotransmitters laypersons are most familiar with.

Like the amines norepinephrine and dopamine, serotonin is synthesized in several different locations in the brain as well as in the intestinal wall and in blood vessels. One of the major producers of this neurotransmitter is a structure in the brainstem called the raphe nucleus. Pathways from the raphe nucleus lead to such diverse structures as the cortex, the hypothalamus, and the hippocampus. It is not surprising then to discover that serotonin appears also to be involved in (and is being used to treat) such diverse disorders as anxiety, obsessive-compulsive disorder, schizophrenia, stroke, obesity, migraine, and nausea (Borne, 1994).

Acetylcholine. Acetylcholine is the only major neurotransmitter that is not derived directly from an amino acid. Its action is generally excitatory, but it can act as an inhibitor, as was shown by Loewi's experiment in which it slowed the heart. Acetylcholine enhances random eye movement (REM) sleep (the phase of sleep when deepest dreaming occurs) and has been shown to be involved in our memory circuits (Hobson, 1989). The degeneration of this neurotransmitter in people who have Alzheimer's disease helps explain the memory loss that usually accompanies this disease (Restak, 1994). Like the amine neurotransmitters, acetylcholine originates in subcortical structures just above the brainstem but is employed at many synapses throughout the brain. The cells of the motor cortex and neurons of the sympathetic nervous system both use acetylcholine to operate all voluntary and many involuntary muscles.

Peptides

During the late 1970s and the 1980s, more than 50 peptides (some researchers estimate there are more than 100) were found to be serving dual purposes in the body and the brain.

We're now going to look at an entirely different group of neurotransmitters, which are synthesized differently from amines and play a slightly different role at the synapse. Peptides are either digestive products or hormones. The ones that are pertinent to our discussion, the peptide hormones, are composed of amino acids joined together to form a chain. Some chains are five amino acids long, while others are composed of as many as 39 amino acids. Like all hormones, they are transported from one part of the body to another in the bloodstream. For example, a peptide called angiotensin is involved in thirst. When the body becomes dehydrated, angiotensin is released into the bloodstream, where it binds to a receptor in the kidney, causing the kidney to conserve water.

Many peptides have been found to operate not only in the body, but also in the brain, hence the name neuropeptides. Let's take our previous example of angiotensin. Acting as a hormone, it causes body tissues to conserve fluids. But conservation isn't enough, so the angiotensin acts effectively as a neurotransmitter on the brain, working at certain synapses to create the sensation of thirst. An animal injected with angiotensin will drink and drink even though it is sated with water (Moyers, 1993). Once again, we see how the human body efficiently uses the same substance for varied purposes. During the late 1970s and the 1980s, researchers found more than 50 peptides (some researchers estimate there are more than 100) that were serving dual purposes in the body and the brain (Gregory, 1987). The peptide hormones function principally as modulators; rather than acting on their own to stimulate or inhibit, they facilitate this action in other neurotransmitters.

A neuron may use one or more modulatory neuropeptides along with several neurotransmitters (Restak, 1994).

Neuropeptides were first discovered in Scotland by a pair of drug addiction researchers, John Hughes and Hans Kosterlitz, in 1975. They were searching for an internally produced chemical that would fit into existing opiate receptor cells. The fact that the body contains receptors for opiates was established a few years earlier by Solomon Snyder and Candace Pert, working at Johns Hopkins University. What Hughes and Kosterlitz discovered was a natural substance that acts much like morphine in blocking pain and producing euphoria. They dubbed this substance "enkephalin," Greek for "in the head." Enkephalins also act in the intestines by regulating the movement of food through the digestive pathway (Pert, 1997).

Endorphins. Additional internal (or endogenous) neuropeptides similar to enkephalins have been identified and lumped together loosely under the generic term "endorphins." The name endorphin is a contraction of "endogenous morphine." When you think about it, it makes sense: Morphine could not produce the analgesic, tranquillizing, and euphoric effects it has if we didn't have a receptor site in the brain for a natural substance that deadens pain and produces euphoria. The brain (as far as we know) does not have receptor sites for poppy plants. But the human brain, as well as the brains of all higher vertebrates, does have receptor sites for its own opiates, and morphine—mimicking this natural substance—slips into these sites.

Why would the brain have opiate receptors? What would be the purpose in having a reward center in the brain? There must be some value for survival, or the opiate receptors (concentrated in the spinal cord, the brainstem, the ventral tegmental area, and the nucleus accumbens) would not have been conserved across the evolutionary scale (Ackerman, 1992). Many scientists believe the answer lies in a reward or pleasure pathway, a neural network

Morphine could not produce the analgesic, tranquillizing, and euphoric effects it has if we didn't have a receptor site in the brain for a natural substance that deadens pain and produces euphoria.

in the middle of the brain that prompts good feelings in response to certain behaviors, such as relieving hunger, quenching thirst, engaging in sex, and escaping from a potentially dangerous situation. In other words, it appears that the brain produces opiate-type neurotransmitters to reinforce those behaviors that are essential for the survival of the individual and of the species. Now we can begin to understand one of the roles of endorphins (as well as of other neurotransmitters such as dopamine, norepinephrine, and serotonin) and the reinforcing effects they have on the reward pathway. Endorphin levels rise in the brain during prolonged, sustained exercise such as running a marathon—or running away from a saber-toothed tiger. Beta-endorphin, a type of endorphin, also increases significantly during childbirth (Fajardo et al., 1994). If pain levels were not reduced, the probability of having a second child would certainly decrease. Positive social contacts, humor, and music also have been shown to increase levels of this group of opiate neuropeptides (Levinthal, 1988). It appears, then, that those behaviors that increase the likelihood of survival are chemically reinforced in the brain.

Other Neuropeptides. Numerous other neuropeptides are not as well known as the enkephalins and the endorphins. Substance P is a neuropeptide present in sensory neurons. When these neurons are stimulated they transmit a message to the higher parts of the brain (those concerned with pain sensation and responses to these sensations) that painful stimulation has occurred. You've probably experienced the effects of this neuropeptide because substance P is present in tooth pulp. Endorphins are thought to block the actions of substance P at the synapse, lessening the awareness of pain. Another neuropeptide, vasopressin, regulates the motility of the intestines, but it can act as a neurotransmitter as well. Cortisol, which will be discussed later in the section on emotions and learning, is still another neuropeptide with powerful effects on the brain and the body.

The Mind-Body Connection

You may have noticed that many of the same peptide modulators occur both in the brain and in the gastrointestinal tract. In *Receptors*, Richard Restak states, "Our 'gut feelings' are more than mere metaphor . . . . The mental and the physical, the mind, the brain, and the body, are intrinsically linked by means of these chemicals." (Restak, 1994, p. 206.) Candace Pert in her book, *Molecules of Emotion*, suggests that because most, if not all, neuropeptides have the ability to change our mood, we may have the capacity to alter our own physiology without drugs. She states:

> Peptides serve to weave the body's organs and systems into a single web that reacts to both internal and external environmental changes with complex, subtly orchestrated responses. Peptides are the sheet music containing the notes, phrases, and rhythms that allow the orchestra—your body—to play as an integrated entity (Pert, 1997, p. 148).

We know that the brain is not sitting in the head totally separated from the rest of the body. The two are inextricably linked in many ways. The neurotransmitters that allow our neurons to communicate are made up of amino acids, which we obtain from the foods we eat. This fact gives new meaning to the saying, "You are what you eat." We all know that we can make ourselves physically ill by worry and stress. Psychosomatic illness (in which mental disorders are manifested in physical symptoms) has been documented for many years. Alternative or complementary medicine is beginning to gain wider credibility and acceptance. We will see in later chapters why this is so, and how exercise, sleep, stress, and mental attitude impact our brain's ability to process information. We are just beginning to understand the mind-body connection. What implications may this fascinating new area of research have for teaching and learning?

"Our 'gut feelings' are more than mere metaphor . . . the mental and the physical, the mind, the brain, and the body, are intrinsically linked by means of these chemicals."

We know that the brain is not sitting in the head totally separated from the rest of the body. The two are inextricably linked in many ways.

Understanding Addiction

A chemical substance synthesized in our brain is called a neurotransmitter. One that is synthesized in a laboratory is called a drug. Often, neurotransmitters and drugs are similar in their molecular composition. We've already seen how one drug, morphine, is able to modulate pain and pleasure by mimicking (or fitting into the receptor sites) for one class of our brain's own chemical substances, the endorphins. Is the same thing true for other drugs, especially the ones frequently used for recreational purposes such as cocaine, amphetamines, and heroin? Basically, the answer is yes, but with a few differences, depending on the drug we're discussing. Most drugs operate the way they do by either fitting into a natural neurotransmitter's receptor site or by modulating the effects of the neurotransmitter in some way.

Earlier, in discussing the effects of endorphins in the brain, we pointed out that many scientists believe there is a pleasure or reward pathway in the brain. It is now time to look at this circuit more closely. Two structures appear to be heavily involved in the brain's reward system. The ventral tegmental area (VTA), as you may remember, is a group of dopamine-producing cells deep in the center of the brain. The dopamine neurons in the VTA are connected by a bridge of fibers to the second brain structure that mediates the pleasure response, the nucleus accumbens. (One group of scientists believe that eventually all pleasure comes down to dopamine. This neurotransmitter has indeed been shown to bind to many receptors in the emotional center of the brain.) When a drug such as cocaine, amphetamine, morphine, or heroin reaches the brain, it acts by inhibiting dopamine reuptake in the VTA, effectively causing more dopamine to remain in the synapse. The excess of dopamine overstimulates the nucleus accumbens, producing a pleasure response. The user can sustain this pleasurable feeling by taking more of the drug (Restak, 1994).

If a chemical substance is synthesized in our brain, we call it a neurotransmitter. If it is synthesized in a laboratory, it's called a drug.

When laboratory rats are hooked to an apparatus that allows them to push a lever that will deliver cocaine or amphetamine directly to the VTA, they press the lever almost continuously, ignoring food and drink and ceasing all other normal activity. The same thing holds true for the opiates heroin and morphine. (Heroin is a derivative of morphine.) Humans appear not to behave much differently from the rats. Virtually all drugs abused by humans, including opiates, amphetamine, cocaine, alcohol, and nicotine, lead to increased levels of dopamine in the nucleus accumbens. Cocaine acts directly on the pleasure centers, producing the user's "high," which helps to explain why it is one of the most addictive substances known (Restak, 1994). Figure 4.3 is a list of some common drugs and the effects they have at the synapse.

Just because a drug mimics one of the brain's own neurotransmitters, it does not necessarily have the same effect. The brain generally controls just how much of a neurotransmitter to release into the synapse, how long to leave it there, and when to dispose of it. Drugs, however, overwhelm this natural functioning, flooding all the synapses and often causing effects quite different from the transmitters they mimic. Even if the drug is one that is prescribed for the treatment of a disorder, the dosage is difficult to regulate. L-dopa (which enhances dopamine development) is often administered to relieve some of the effects of Parkinson's disease. Too little of this drug, however, and the symptoms remain; too much, and the patient often displays characteristics of schizophrenia such as hallucinations and paranoia.

Why do people take illicit drugs? The reasons vary, but in some instances drug use may be the result of abnormalities in the chemical balance of the brains. Studies at Harvard Medical School determined that some cases of depression are the result of low levels of dopamine in the brain. Often, afflicted persons aren't aware of the cause of their depression; they only know that cocaine or amphetamine makes them feel better. For others, the

Cocaine acts directly on the pleasure centers, producing the user's "high," which helps to explain why it is one of the most addictive substances known.

Just because a drug mimics one of the brain's own neurotransmitters, it does not necessarily have the same effect.

risk for drug addiction may be caused by a higher than normal level of dopamine. For these persons, cocaine augments the natural high (Restak, 1994).

This discussion of addiction may not appear to have much relevance for the average educator. When we consider that the reward pathway in the brain was designed for good reasons, however, and that the "natural" sources of reward (feelings of being liked, being successful or productive, and feeling attractive) are often not present in students' lives, we can begin to understand why they are drawn to substances that increase pleasure. An effective classroom climate might be described as one that allows students to naturally increase the endorphin, dopamine, norepinephrine, or serotonin levels in their brains, making the students' education experiences more pleasurable and rewarding.

An effective classroom climate might be described as a climate that allows students to naturally increase the endorphin, dopamine, norepinephrine, or serotonin levels in their brains, making the students' education experiences more pleasurable and rewarding.

~ Figure 4.3 ~ DRUGS AND WHERE THEY REACT	
Drug	**Where it Reacts**
Alcohol	Along with barbituates, alcohol decreases the release of GABA.
Cocaine and amphetamine	These drugs block dopamine and norephinephrine reuptake channels.
Heroin and morphine	Morphine and heroin (a derivative of morphine) mimic the natural endorphins.
Nicotine	Nicotine activates receptors on hippocampal cells that typically respond to acetylcholine.
Prozac (Paxil, Zoloft)	These antidepressant drugs block serotonin reuptake channels.

Synapse Strengtheners

1. In your own words, see if you can explain to a person who has not read this chapter why information processing in the brain is both electrical and chemical.

2. With the book closed, draw a diagram of a synapse between two neurons, labeling the following parts: presynaptic neuron, postsynaptic neuron, synaptic cleft, vesicles, molecules of a neurotransmitter, and receptors. Open the book and check your drawing for accuracy. (Artistic ability doesn't count!)

3. Design a lesson to teach your students about the chemical basis of addiction.

4. If you are reading this book as a part of a study group, discuss how the information in this chapter relates to classroom climate and what teachers can do to decrease the likelihood of students' involvement with illicit drugs.

PART II

From Sensory Input to Information Storage

We know more about why certain activities and strategies are more effective than others in increasing student understanding.

We can study the brain through many different lenses. In Part I we looked at the anatomy (the structure) and physiology (the function) of the brain. Whereas an understanding of the parts of the brain and how they operate is important, it doesn't tell us how these parts work together to allow us to receive information; to discard what is irrelevant; or to store or recall information we've seen, heard, and thought. How does the brain create the elusive qualities we call mind and memory? Studying the brain by analyzing its anatomy is a fascinating field of study, but it is limited. To further our understanding, we need another way to view the brain.

Part II looks at the brain through the lens of an information-processing model. This model can add to our knowledge base by helping us understand what roles specific brain structures play in the complex acts of receiving, processing, storing, and retrieving information. Here we begin to discuss the classroom implications and applications of the research. Some of the theoretical base and research for this section comes not from neuroscience but from the fields of cognitive psychology and educational research. Though much of this research is not new, it takes on new meaning when viewed from a neurological perspective. For example, the concept of "transfer" has a long research history. Many classroom studies have documented the effect of prior knowledge on new learning—often called *positive or negative transfer*. Our comprehension of the concept is increased, however, when we understand its neurological underpinnings.

Information is not stored in a specific location in the brain but in various locations—visual, auditory, and motor cortices—and is joined in circuits or networks of neurons. When we experience something new, the brain "looks" for an existing network into which the new information will fit. If the fit is good, what was learned/stored previously gives meaning to the new information and we will have *positive transfer*. If the new information is similar in some aspect but not a complete fit, *negative transfer* may occur. The concept is the same whether explained by an educational researcher or a neuroscientist; however, as a teacher, I now know not only that positive or negative transfer occurs, but I have a better understanding of why it occurs. This additional information increases my knowledge base and allows me to articulate to my students, their parents, and perhaps even to policy-makers why certain activities and strategies are more effective than others in increasing student understanding of the concepts I am teaching.

5

Sensory Memory: Getting Information into the Brain

What is memory, and how does it relate to the learning process? We commonly view memory as a "thing," and we talk about how poor our memory is or how good someone else's memory is. In education, memorizing information is often viewed as poor practice. Viewed in this way, memory indeed seems to be too narrow a topic to begin a discussion of how the brain processes information. If we think about what life would be without memory, however, our perception changes somewhat. Those who have lost their memory have lost much of what makes them who they are. What makes us unique, what determines to a large degree who we become, is our ability to acquire and store new information. Out of that ability come new concepts, new ideas, new feelings, and ultimately our behaviors. Memory is what enables us to learn by experience. In fact, memory is essential to survival. Without the ability to learn, store, and recall how we should respond to environmental dangers, knowing when to run or fight and even how to run or fight, the individual has small chance of survival. Seen in this light, the understanding of memory becomes vitally important to us as parents and educators. Little formal distinction exists between learning and memory; the two are so inextricably linked that a study of one becomes a study of the other.

74

Metaphors for Memory

Human memory is invisible and intangible; we must consider it a *process*, not a thing. In an effort to describe memory, historically we have explained it in terms of metaphors. Over time, three major metaphors have evolved. One views memory as a kind of intellectual muscle; the more you use it, the stronger it becomes. According to this view, the hours spent in memorizing lines of poetry, dates of wars, and Latin phrases strengthen the mind and make it better able to remember any and all other kinds of material. This is not necessarily true; in fact, extensive memorizing of material may even decrease the ability to memorize additional information (Underwood, 1968).

Another popular metaphor for memory has its origin in the writings of Plato, who likened the mind to a tablet of wax on which impressions are made. In this view, rehearsing experiences or information strengthens or deepens the impressions, resulting in information that is more easily remembered. While this metaphor may seem to fit with many of our own experiences (rehearsing the multiplication tables or rules of spelling such as "I before E"), it doesn't explain why we have vivid recollections of emotional events we experienced only once, or why when we rehearse all items in a list equally, we remember the first and last items more readily than those in the middle. It appears that the reasons for remembering and forgetting are more complex than repetitions of experiences.

As an example of this complexity, Daniel J. Siegel at the University of California, Los Angeles, and author of *The Developing Mind*, asks his audiences to picture the Eiffel Tower in their "mind's eye." He states that his voice creates sound waves that vibrate the tympanic membranes in the listeners' ears. Those sound waves in turn are transformed into electrical impulses by the Organ of Corti and forwarded to the temporal lobes for

Memory is what enables us to learn by experience. In fact, memory is essential to survival.

decoding. Next, the information is sent to the occipital lobes for visual processing. The inputs from these two parts of the brain are integrated, and the listener is able to "see" or remember the Eiffel Tower. Siegel states that the listeners reactivated a neural network that had previously been established when at some point they had seen the Eiffel Tower or a picture of it (Siegel, 2000).

In 1949 Donald Hebb, a visionary psychologist, proposed a similar theory in his book, *The Organization of Behavior*. He proposed that neurons that fire together simultaneously are more likely to fire together again in the future (Greenfield, 1997). Siegel colorfully rephrases what is known as Hebb's "law" when he states, "Neurons that fire together, survive together and wire together" (Siegel, 2000). Many neuroscientists concur that this is probably the physiological basis for memory: Experience changes the way synaptic connections are made and increases the probability of firing in a predictable association with other neurons.

"Neurons that fire together, survive together and wire together."

An Introduction to the Model

For the past several decades, the predominant model of memory has been an information-processing model. Growing out of information-processing theory, it became popular at about the same time as, or perhaps as a result of, the invention of the computer. Many variations on this model are the result of new understanding gained from many fields, including neuroscience, cognitive psychology, and developmental psychology. Figure 5.1 shows this model.

The diagram in Figure 5.1, which provides an organizing framework for human memory, should be viewed as a representation of the *functional* (rather than structural) properties of the human memory system. In other words, this model does not imply that these three broad categories of memory are located in different areas of the brain, nor is it meant to imply that they are separate, autonomous systems. Furthermore, the three categories do not represent sharp, distinct stages in the process of memory, but instead they are convenient labels to help us understand the processes by which the human mind encodes, stores, retrieves, and integrates new information with previously stored information. Our starting point in understanding learning and memory is the part of the model we'll call *sensory* memory.

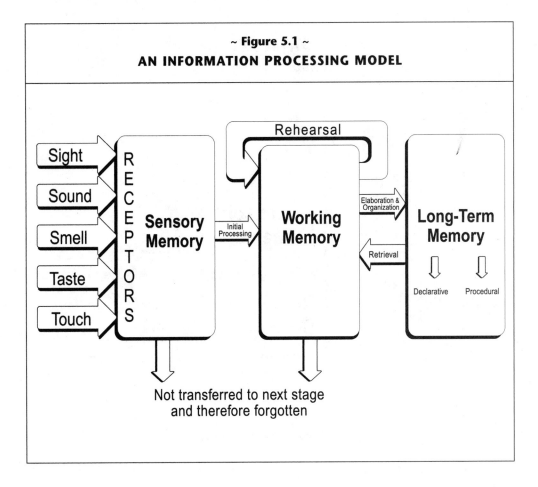

~ **Figure 5.1** ~

AN INFORMATION PROCESSING MODEL

Sensory Memory

Figure 5.2 illustrates the beginning part of the model, sensory memory. It might more accurately be labeled "sensory store," "sensory buffers," or even "sensory perception." Everything in memory begins as a sensory input from the environment. The role of sensory memory is to take the information coming into the brain through the sensory receptors and hold it for a fraction of a second until a decision is made about what to do with it.

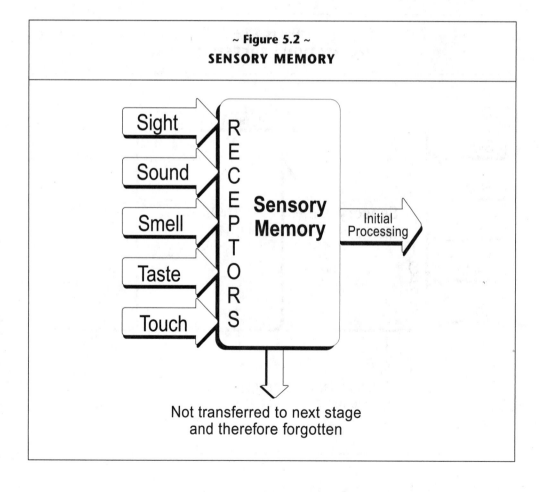

~ **Figure 5.2** ~
SENSORY MEMORY

The process is fairly straightforward. A light ray hits the retina of the eye and forms a brief memory (an *iconic* memory) with a duration of milliseconds. It is probably best understood as a prolongation of the original stimulus trace required to allow time for recognition and further processing to take place. According to Joseph Torgesen, professor at Florida State University, the same is probably true of the other senses (Torgesen, 1996). One exception may be auditory stimuli. Auditory signals also are recorded briefly in what is usually referred to as *echoic* memory. There is some evidence that echoic traces may last a little longer, perhaps as long as 20 seconds (Gazzaniga, Ivry, & Mangun, 1998).

But even though the process seems relatively simple, a problem arises because this sensory input does not arrive one piece at a time as separate bits of information, but rather it arrives simultaneously. During any fractional moment in time, an enormous amount of sensory stimuli is bombarding our bodies, giving us much more information than we can possibly attend to. If you were consciously aware of all the images, sounds, tactile sensations, tastes, and smells that were simultaneously impinging upon your body, you would experience sensory overload. Without some mechanism for organizing this raw sensory data into a meaningful pattern, you would not be able to function. There has to be some provision for discarding irrelevant data. The role of filtering the enormous amount of information entering the senses is what we are calling sensory memory.

The brain is sometimes referred to as a sponge that soaks up information. A better metaphor would be a sieve: By some estimates, 99 percent of all sensory information is discarded almost immediately upon entering the brain (Gazzaniga, 1998). The reason the brain filters out such vast amounts of information is that much of it is irrelevant. There would normally be little functional or survival value in remembering what your clothes felt like on your body a few minutes ago or how a pen felt in your hand

The role of sensory memory is to take the information coming into the brain through the sensory receptors and hold it for a fraction of a second until a decision is made about what to do with it.

The brain is sometimes referred to as a sponge that soaks up information. But a better metaphor would be a sieve: By some estimates, 99 percent of all sensory information is discarded almost immediately upon entering the brain.

when you were writing a week ago. The question under consideration is how the brain decides what to keep and what to discard. What factors influence the brain to pay attention to certain stimuli and not others?

From Sensory Signals to Perceptions

All information received by sensory receptors needs to be sent to the appropriate sensory cortex to be processed. As you may remember from Chapter 2, the organ that plays a major role in this transfer is the thalamus. All sensory data, except smells, travel first to the thalamus. From there the data are relayed to the specific portion of the cortex designated to process sight, sound, taste, or touch. A discussion of the complex physiology by which this happens is beyond the scope of this book, but it is important to understand that as information travels from the sensory receptors to the site where it is processed, it is, in a sense, transformed. It changes from a photon of light or a sound wave into a percept. In other words, we do not "see" the photon of light or the sound wave per se, we *perceive* a figure or a sound, and the perception is uniquely shaped by that perceiving mind at that moment.

Perception refers to the meaning we attach to information as it is received through the senses. Our eyes may capture an image in much the same way as a camera, but what we see (or perceive) is influenced by the information we have stored in our brains. For example, look at the following figure: ℬ. If you were asked what *number* this is, you would probably say "13." But if you were asked to name the *letter*, your answer might be "B." The figure didn't change; your perception changed based on what you were asked and your knowledge of numbers and letters. To a young child who had no stored information of either numbers or letters, these would be meaningless marks on the paper. The assignment of meaning to incoming stimuli, therefore, depends on prior knowledge and on what we expect to see. In a sense, the

Our eyes may capture an image in much the same way as a camera, but what we see (or perceive) is influenced by the information we already have stored in our brains.

brain checks the existing neural networks of information to see if the new information is something that activates a previously stored neural network. (We'll look at the physiology of how neural networks are formed in a later chapter.) This matching of new input to stored information is called pattern recognition and is a critical aspect of attention. Pattern recognition works so well that you are able to recognize a letter no matter whether it is printed *ℬ, b* or Ƀ . But if you had never seen a *b* before and did not know what it represented, it would be meaningless, because there would be no recognition or match.

The assignment of meaning to incoming stimuli depends on prior knowledge and on what we expect to see.

From Perception to Attention

Children are often criticized for "not paying attention." There is no such thing as not paying attention; the brain is always paying attention to something. What we really mean is that the child or student is not paying attention to what we think is relevant or important. Attention, as all of us know, is selective.

What are the factors that influence whether a stimulus is kept or dropped? Why is it that two persons can experience the same sensory input but one attends to one stimulus and the other attends to a totally different element of the input? It is important to be aware that in this initial processing stage we're not talking about a consciously driven process. While it is true that with conscious effort we are able to direct and sustain our attention on a specific stimulus, most of the time this is not the case. It would be inefficient and perhaps impossible in everyday life to consciously determine what we were going to focus on at every given moment. The brain is constantly scanning the environment for stimuli. This is done largely by automatic mechanisms. As you may recall from Chapter 2, the reticular activating system (RAS) plays an important role in filtering the thousands of stimuli, in excluding trivial information, and in focusing on relevant data. In other words, most of the time your "unconscious" brain is tak-

There is no such thing as not paying attention; the brain is always paying attention to something.

ing over the initial decision-making process for you. What factors influence the brain during this initial filtering of information? How does it determine what is relevant and what is not?

One key component in the filtering process is whether the incoming stimulus is different from what we are used to seeing—whether it is novel. Novelty is an innate attention-getter. To survive, our remote ancestors living on the savannahs or in caves had to be aware of any novel or unique stimulus present in the environment. We're not much different. Our brains today are still programmed to pay attention to the unusual, such as a detour sign when we're driving. Teachers often take advantage of this phenomenon by providing information in a surprising or novel manner. Coming to class dressed in the costume of a historical character or giving the students balloons to introduce a lesson on air pressure are examples.

However, a characteristic of novelty that makes it difficult to employ on a daily basis is the brain's tendency toward habituation. If a sight or sound is new and unusual, we initially pay close attention. But if this same sight or sound occurs over and over, the brain normally becomes so accustomed to the stimulus that it ignores it. This is what is known as habituation. If you have ever lived near an airport, chances are you reached a point where you seldom paid attention to the jets taking off or landing. You cannot avoid hearing a nearby Boeing 747 taking off, but after the same sound is repeated day after day, it is no longer novel and is filtered out by the sensory system as not important. A woman may not notice her own perfume, while others do: Her olfactory receptors have become habituated to the aroma, but a person who is unfamiliar with the fragrance probably will notice it.

The intensity of stimuli is another factor that affects attention. Generally, the louder a sound or the brighter a light, the more likely each is to draw attention. When two stimuli are competing for attention, the one that is more intense will attract attention

One key component in the filtering process is whether the incoming stimulus is different from what we are used to seeing—whether it is novel.

first. Advertisers take advantage of this phenomenon by increasing the volume of television commercials to obtain our attention.

A third factor influencing attention is movement. In general, our attention is directed toward stimuli that move. The illusion of movement can be produced by blinking neon signs that attract attention more readily than signs that do not blink. The flashing lights on police cars are another example of using movement as an attention-getting device.

At this point we are talking about the processing taking place during the initial presentation of stimuli to the sensory receptors. This processing is largely unconscious and, for the most part, out of our control. As we have seen, however, it is possible to influence what the brain pays attention to by using novelty, intensity, or movement. In the classroom it is probable, however, that none of these will prove useful over time because of habituation. Flicking the light switch to get students' attention may work well the first few times, but with extended use, students often will fail to notice or respond to this signal. In the same vein, raising your voice level may get attention for a while but often results in students raising their voice levels to match yours. A novel event is only novel for a short time. So does this mean that teachers and parents have little influence on what their students' or children's brains home in on? Are we at the mercy of a capricious brain that resists all efforts to get it to focus on a particular stimulus? In a word, no. Two factors strongly influence whether the brain initially attends to arriving information and whether this attention will be sustained. These two factors are meaning and emotion, and over these we do have some control.

In other words, the neural networks "check out" sensory stimuli as soon as they enter the brain to see if they form a familiar pattern.

Meaning and Attention

Earlier in this chapter, we discussed pattern recognition. This phenomenon describes how the brain attempts to match incoming sensory stimuli with information is already stored in circuits or networks of neurons. In other words, the neural networks "check out" sensory stimuli as soon as they enter the brain to see if they form a familiar pattern. If they do, a match occurs, and the brain determines that the new visual stimuli are familiar. In this case, we could say that the new information makes sense or has meaning. What happens if there is no match? The brain may attend to the meaningless information for a short time because it is novel; but if it can make no sense out of the incoming stimuli, the brain will probably not process them further.

Think about picking up a book in the waiting room of an office while you're waiting for an appointment. You open the cover and discover that the book is written in a language you don't read. You will probably put the book down rather quickly and look around for something to read that you *can* understand. Or imagine trying to read a document full of charts, graphs, or formulas that make no sense even if they are in your language. Sustained attention on something that you can't figure out or that makes no sense is not only boring, it's almost impossible. I'm afraid that too often we expect this feat of our children and our students.

Look at the illustration in Figure 5.3 (Hunt, 1982). You may have some difficulty at first seeing anything but spots. With a little diligence, you will eventually see the image of a dog, more specifically, the image of a dalmatian. (Here's a hint: the dalmatian is a bit to the right of center. Its head is pointing down and it is sniffing the ground or drinking from a puddle. It is headed somewhat away from you.) Once you've seen the dog, it will be difficult not to see it. It is almost impossible to draw an outline around the whole dog, yet you can discern it nonetheless.

Think about what just happened in your brain. Even though you cannot see the entire dog, your brain used what information was there to allow you to recognize it. What is necessary for this to occur? Remember the example cited earlier about being able

Sustained attention on something that you can't figure out that makes no sense is not only boring, it's almost impossible.

to see the Eiffel Tower in your "mind's eye"? You were able to "see" it because you activated a previously established circuit of neurons in which that information was stored. The same thing is true in the case of the photograph of the dalmatian. You would never be able to detect this dog among the spots if you had never seen one or a picture of one and it were not already stored in your brain. You cannot reconstruct or reactivate a neural circuit or network if it was never activated in the first place.

~ Figure 5.3 ~

Source: Attributed to Ronald C. James. Published in *The Universe Within*, by Morton Hunt, 1982, New York, Simon & Schuster, p. 72.

We can now begin to understand the term "meaning" and the important role it plays in attention. If our brains can find no previously activated networks into which the new information fits, they are much less likely to attend to it. Our species has not survived by attending to and storing meaningless information.

Consider students in a classroom confronted with information that doesn't match anything they've previously stored. Their brains look for an appropriate network to help them make sense or meaning of this information. If nothing can be found, the information is discarded as meaningless. Without being facetious, is it possible that much of what we teach in schools fits this description, and we shouldn't be surprised that our students' brains often refuse to attend? In later chapters we'll discuss various strategies that can be employed to make information more meaningful, but at this point let's move on to a second factor that has an equal (if not greater) impact on attention.

Emotion and Attention

In his talks to educators, Robert Sylwester, author of *A Celebration of Neurons*, often states, "Emotion drives attention, and attention drives learning." To a large degree, this appears to be true. Understanding why will require us to look more carefully at several subcortical structures that control our emotional responses (Sylwester, 1995).

Recall that the brain is constantly scanning its environment, sifting and sorting through the incoming information to determine what to keep and what to ignore. Why does this occur? Because it is essential for the survival of the individual and the species. Think about it: If a dangerous animal were charging toward you and your brain decided to focus on its rate of speed or taxonomic classification, you wouldn't be around later to pass on your genes. It is imperative that we possess a system that sepa-

You cannot reconstruct or reactivate a neural circuit or network if it was never activated in the first place.

rates the essential from the frivolous in a short time, and we do. At one time this system was called the "limbic system." This term has proved to be somewhat limiting and perhaps even inaccurate. Scientists disagree about which structures make up this system and, more importantly, disagree over whether it is even a system. Perhaps the terminology isn't that important. What is important is that a group of structures work together to assist us in focusing on those aspects of environmental input that are critical to our survival.

Our species has not survived by attending to and storing meaningless information.

The first player in the process is the thalamus. It is a sort of relay station that receives the incoming information and sends it to the appropriate part of the cortex for further processing. At the same time, however, the information is also sent to the amygdala. It is as if the message is duplicated so that it can be sent simultaneously to different areas of the brain. Why are our brains designed for this type of parallel processing? As you may recall from the earlier discussion of the amygdala, the role it plays is to determine the emotional relevance of the incoming stimuli. Is this something that could hurt me or something I like? Do I run away from it or toward it? Conversely, the role of the cortex is to process the incoming stimuli rationally, to place it in context to make sense of it, and to decide on a course of action.

The brain is biologically programmed to attend first to information that has strong emotional content.

It may not come as a surprise that the pathway from the thalamus to the amygdala is much shorter than the pathway from the thalamus to the cortex. In fact, the thalamus/amygdala pathway is one synapse long, allowing the amygdala to receive the information approximately a quarter of a second sooner than the cortex (LeDoux, 1996). The cortex provides a more accurate representation of the stimulus, but it takes much longer to do so. If there is potential danger, time is of the essence. In his book *The Emotional Brain*, Joseph LeDoux calls the thalamus/amygdala pathway the "quick and dirty route," which signifies the often less-than-rational response the brain makes in emotional situa-

Educators need to be aware of the processes the brain uses during this initial sifting and sorting stage.

tions. Understanding this unconscious emotional response system (the quick and dirty route) also helps explain the less-than-rational reactions we sometimes observe in our students when they are confronted with situations their brains perceive to be emotionally attention-getting.

The brain is biologically programmed to attend first to information that has strong emotional content. (It is also programmed to remember this information longer, a phenomenon we'll examine in the next chapter.) Our brains and our students' brains are designed to pay attention not only to physical dangers in the environment, but to facial expressions and other components of body language that contain emotional information necessary for survival in our culture. Consider the social problems of autistic children, who generally lack the ability to read these cues.

In this chapter we've looked at the first step in information processing or, to put it another way, the first step in memory and learning. All the stimuli constantly bombarding our senses find their way into our brains, but little of them remains there. Educators need to be aware of the processes the brain uses during this initial sifting and sorting stage. Cognizance of the roles meaning and emotion play is critical to understanding why the brain pays attention to some stimuli and not to others. If students are not paying attention, they are not engaged; and, hence, they are not learning. In the next chapter we'll look at how we can consciously use meaning and emotion to enhance student learning.

If students are not paying attention, they are not engaged; and, hence, they are not learning.

Synapse Strengtheners

1. Suppose a colleague of yours complains that her students don't pay attention. How could you help her understand some of the reasons this appears to be the case?

2. In a small blank book or tablet, begin a Reflection Journal by writing one or two paragraphs on the role emotion plays in attention and learning.

3. In your study group, discuss what makes something meaningful to the brain. You might also want to discuss whether your present curriculum has inherent meaning or if you may need to find ways to make it more meaningful.

6

Working Memory:
The Conscious Processing
of Information

W ithin the human cortex lies a critical part of the secret of human consciousness. Here is found our ability to be aware of what we are seeing and hearing, to use language to communicate with one another, to conjure up stored visual images and describe them, and other abilities considered to be the unique domain of the human brain. As you will recall from Chapter 5, not all information processing is conscious; in fact, most of it is not. The brain is constantly taking in sensory stimuli from the outside world, assembling and sorting the stimuli, discarding much of the information, and directing only some of it to our conscious attention. Although consciousness represents a small part of information processing, without it we could not remember an unfamiliar phone number long enough to dial it or recall the first part of a sentence as we are reading its end.

Although it is important, the ability to hold small amounts of information is transient and short term. We generally forget an unfamiliar phone number as soon as we dial it; and most of us would be unable to repeat the exact words of a sentence that contained more than a few words. Figure 6.1 depicts this short-term processing ability by the box labeled "Working Memory." The arrow leading from sensory memory to working memory represents that portion of sensory data that captures the brain's atten-

Although consciousness represents a small part of information processing, without it we could not remember an unfamiliar phone number long enough to dial it or recall the first part of a sentence as we are reading its end.

tion well enough that it allows you to become consciously aware of it. The arrow from long-term memory to working memory shows that the contents of working memory may also include information retrieved from long-term memory. The arrow going in the opposite direction from working memory to long-term memory represents our ability to store for a longer period of time information we've been working with consciously.

Again, we should use this model with caution. As discussed in the last chapter, we should view this diagram as a representation

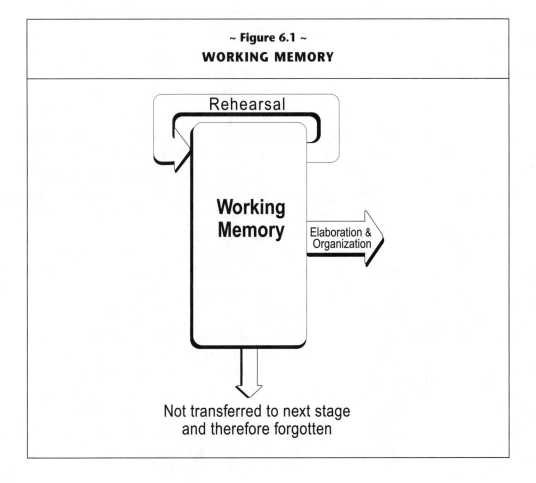

~ Figure 6.1 ~
WORKING MEMORY

Rehearsal

Working Memory

Elaboration & Organization

Not transferred to next stage and therefore forgotten

of the *functional* rather than *structural* properties of the human memory system. None of the three broad divisions of human memory is a separate, dedicated storage area in a particular region of the brain. This model summarizes the broad range of memory phenomena from the perspective of information processing. Most scientists agree that memory is a multifaceted, complex process that involves activating a large number of neural circuits in many areas of the brain. There is no uniform agreement, however, on a model that accurately represents these many facets. Some researchers view short-term memory and working memory as different processes; others consider working memory as a part of short-term memory. Some cognitive scientists do not believe that working memory and long-term memory are totally separate; they believe that working memory is best conceptualized as a portion of long-term memory that is temporarily activated (Wagner, 1996). This is similar to Hebb's view that memory represents continued activity or reverberation of the neural cells involved in perception. Today, the majority of scientists seem to prefer the term "working memory" to the older "short-term memory," as it better characterizes the many complex activities that it represents. (Both sensory and working memory are of short duration, so in a sense they could both be considered "short-term.")

Working memory allows us to integrate current perceptual information with stored knowledge, and to consciously manipulate the information (think about it, talk about it, and rehearse it) well enough to ensure its storage in long-term memory. We should not think of working memory solely as a conduit to long-term memory, however; much incoming sensory information is needed only temporarily and is then discarded. Working memory appears to serve other purposes as well. Cognitive psychologist B. F. Pennington refers to working memory as a "computational arena," in which information relevant to a current task is both maintained on line and subject to further processing

(Pennington, cited in Torgesen, 1996). An example of the computational function of working memory would be what happens when you do mental arithmetic such as 24 x 8 = 192. In addition, working memory is involved in such higher cognitive "executive functions" as planning, organizing, and rehearsing. Think of working memory as the CEO of a company, who keeps track of who does what and makes sure everything gets done.

Although working memory appears to reside in multiple locations in the brain, depending on the task it is given, many scientists believe that the frontal lobe (specifically the prefrontal cortex) is the primary location of activity (Bear et al., 1996; Gazzaniga et al., 1998). The National Institute of Mental Health (NIMH) recently conducted studies using fMRI technology to scan the brains of subjects as they were involved in seeing a face or series of letters, holding the information briefly, then recalling it. The imaging revealed increased activity in the prefrontal cortex. When the investigators gave the subjects increasingly longer strings of numbers to remember, the prefrontal brain areas distinguished themselves by working harder as the load became more complex (NIMH, 1997). A 1998 study by NIMH's James Haxby and Susan Courtney revealed specialized circuitry for spatial working memory in the frontal cortex. An example of this system would be keeping track of the ever-changing locations of other cars while you're driving.

Studies of patients with lesions in the frontal lobes have highlighted another function of this area: the shaping of present behavior and the ability to carry out plans. Antonio Damasio (1994), in his book *Descartes' Error*, extensively examines one of the most famous cases of frontal lobe damage. He tells the true story of Phineas Gage, a railroad crew foreman. One day in 1848, Gage was tamping explosive powder into a hole in preparation for blasting when the tamping iron he was holding contacted a rock, and the powder exploded. When the charge went off, it sent the

Most scientists agree that memory is a multifaceted, complex process that involves activating a large number of neural circuits in many areas of the brain.

Working memory allows us to integrate current perceptual information with stored knowledge, and to consciously manipulate the information (think about it, talk about it, and rehearse it) perhaps well enough to ensure its storage in long-term memory.

rod into Gage's head just below his left eye. After passing through his left frontal lobe, it exited the top of his head. Amazingly, Gage survived, but his personality was drastically and permanently altered. Before the accident, he was responsible, respected, and known as a shrewd businessperson. Following the accident, he behaved erratically, had difficulty making decisions or planning ahead, and became much like a recalcitrant child in his social interactions. Damasio proposes that the neural connections between the unconscious body states we call emotion and the conscious processing structures in the frontal lobes (which were severely damaged in Gage's brain) are what allow us to function rationally, plan for the future, and make appropriate cognitive and emotional decisions. Without the circuits and structures that make up working memory, we would be unable to access the emotional connections so critical for rational thought and planning.

Think of working memory as the CEO of a company, who keeps track of who does what and makes sure everything gets done.

The 18-Second Holding Pattern

The capacity of the brain for short-term storage and processing of information is somewhat limited, as teachers have always known. Without rehearsal or constant attention, information remains in working memory for only about 15–20 seconds (McGee & Wilson, 1984). Peterson and Peterson carried out the first systematic study of this phenomenon in 1959 (Gazzaniga et al., 1998). They gave subjects the task of remembering a set of three consonants, such as SVL or XCJ, that had been flashed on a screen for a fraction of a second. As soon as the letters were removed, they instructed the subjects to count backward by threes in time with a metronome. The researchers assumed that this interference task would prevent the subjects from repeating or rehearsing the letters, thus providing an accurate measure of how long unrehearsed information remains in working memory. On different trials, they asked subjects to stop counting and name the consonants after 3, 6, 9, 12, or 18 seconds. At 3 seconds, approximately 20 percent of the subjects had forgotten the consonants, and at 18 seconds, no one could remember them.

Eighteen seconds may seem to be so brief a memory span as to be almost useless, but a closer look suggests that this is efficient. If you could not remember information for at least 18 seconds without rehearsal, you would have already forgotten the words that made up the first part of this sentence and comprehension would be impossible. On the other hand, it would be a disadvantage to remember permanently every word in every sentence you have ever read. A memory system that provides temporary storage of just the right amount of information without overloading itself is indeed efficient. Fortunately, as we will see later in this chapter, strategies exist for retaining information much longer than 18 seconds.

Without rehearsal or constant attention, information remains in working memory for only about 15–20 seconds.

The Cocktail Party Effect

How is it that in the noisy, confusing environment of a cocktail party, where many conversations are occurring, you are able to focus on a single conversation? The brain accomplishes this using selective auditory attention, often referred to as the "cocktail party effect." This allows you to filter out the other, often louder conversations and pay attention to the one that is most relevant. What if you wanted to listen to two conversations simultaneously or wanted your students to pay attention to what you are saying and what they were reading at the same time? Unfortunately, as nice as that would be, in most circumstances it's not possible.

It would be a disadvantage to remember permanently every word in every sentence you have ever read.

British psychologist E. C. Cherry first studied the cocktail party effect in the early 1950s. He analyzed the effect by providing competing speech inputs into each ear using headphones (dichotic listening). He sometimes asked subjects to repeat or "shadow" the train of thought coming into one ear while ignoring a similar input into the other ear. Under these conditions, the subjects could remember little of the unshadowed message (Cherry, 1953). Although the cocktail party effect refers to auditory processing, a similar effect can be observed in visual processing.

The following experiment will allow you to experience this. In Figure 6.2, you will see a group of words. Some of the words are written in bold type and some in light. As quickly as you can, read *only* the words in bold type.

Now that you have finished, recall all you can about the message in bold without looking back. Next, try to recall the words written in light type. Like the subjects in the shadowing experiment, you probably did not recall many of the latter. Even if you recall a word or two, did you notice that the words in light type are the same seven words repeated over and over?

As a parent or teacher, you have no doubt witnessed the cocktail party effect in your child or student and perhaps in yourself as well. It is nearly impossible to consciously process two trains of thought at the same time, especially if they involve the same sensory modality. (When you are talking on the phone and someone in the room wants to give you a message, it is far easier to process the message if it is written rather than spoken.)

It is nearly impossible to consciously process two trains of thought at the same time, especially if they involve the same sensory modality.

~ Figure 6.2 ~
A COCKTAIL PARTY EXPERIMENT

In performing an experiment like this one on man **attention** car **it** house **is** boy **critically** hat **important** shoe **that** candy **the** man **material** car **that** house **is** boy **being** hat **read** shoe **by** candy **the** man **subject** car **for** house **the** boy **relevant** hat **task** shoe **be** candy **cohesive** man **and** car **grammatically** house **correct** boy **but** hat **without** shoe **either** candy **being** man **so** car **easy** house **that** boy **full** hat **attention** shoe **is** candy **not** man **required** car **in** house **order** boy **to** hat **read** shoe **nor too difficult.**

Consider the typical lecture in a class where students are required to take notes. Trying to take coherent notes is a difficult task. If the student begins to think about what the teacher just said, the next input may be missed. Often students write the words on the page but have little conceptual understanding of what they just wrote. If the students don't comprehend what is being said, don't see the relevance, or begin to daydream, none of the lecture is processed. Every teacher has had the experience of saying something to students one day and the next day having students act as if they've never heard it. Now we can begin to understand why this may happen.

Note that *doing* two things at the same time is different from consciously *processing* two inputs at the same time. It is certainly possible to *do* two things at the same time if one of them is automatic. Recall from Chapter 2 that motor neurons (with assistance from the cerebellum) may become so used to being activated in a particular sequence that they fire automatically with little or no conscious processing. When writing has become automatic, it is no longer necessary to consciously determine when to dot an "i" or cross a "t," which allows you to pay attention to the content of your writing. Most of the time you are able to comprehend what you are reading because the decoding process is automatic. First-grade students who are still sounding out most of the words in a sentence and for whom decoding is not automatic, however, will have a difficult time comprehending what they are reading.

Every teacher has had the experience of saying something to students one day and the next day having students act as if they've never heard it.

First-grade students who are still sounding out most of the words in a sentence and for whom decoding is not automatic, however, will have a difficult time comprehending what they are reading.

The Magical Number Seven (Plus or Minus Two)

A second limitation of working memory is one of capacity. In the 1950s, cognitive scientist George Miller conducted studies to determine how much information individuals can process consciously. Miller presented subjects with items to be remembered in groups of varying size. Regardless of the type of information—

words, objects, or numerals—the number of items the subjects retained typically proved to be around seven. Miller described this phenomenon in a paper he titled *The Magical Number Seven, Plus or Minus Two: Some Hints on Our Capacity for Processing Information* (Miller, 1956). Miller's research validated something we've long known intuitively. Think about it: How many digits in a phone number, notes on a scale, or days in a week? Miller referred to this characteristic of human memory as the span of immediate memory.

To test this for yourself, try the following memory-span test. Spend about 7 seconds memorizing the following list of 7 digits: 7 4 3 8 5 9 2. When you have finished, look away and try repeating them in order. If your memory span is average, you probably had no difficulty recalling all of them. Now do the same with the following list of 10 digits, giving yourself 10 seconds to memorize them: 6 7 9 4 5 8 1 3 2 9. Unless you have an unusual memory span, you probably did not do as well on the second list.

Previous studies have shown that the number of items that can be held in working memory varies with age. If a test requires a subject to recall strings of digits like the one in the previous paragraph, the typical child age 5 can recall only two digits, plus or minus two. At age 7, children can recall an average of three digits, and at age 11, the average recall is five digits. The number of digits children can recall accurately increases by one every two years until a mental age of 15. At this age, the normal adult capacity of seven (plus or minus two) is reached (Pascual-Leone, 1970).

We should be cautious, however, in determining the capacity of working memory from tests of digit or word span alone. Working memory is more than a passive storehouse for discrete bits of information. In most learning situations, we are required to hold some bits of information in consciousness while we are manipulating other bits of information that are relevant to the task. Whether reading a passage in a text or solving a mathematical problem, the cognitive activity includes an interplay of processing and storage. Tests of working memory that measure the ability to retain some information, while simultaneously carrying out ongoing processing activities, appear to be more accurate measures of the capacity of working memory in real-life tasks. When these more complex measures are used, we find that age does not predict capacity as reliably as do the difficulty and duration of the task (Towse, Hitch, & Hutton, 1998).

Chunking

Working memory is indeed limited. Still, before we become too discouraged with its space limitations, we need to realize that these limitations can be circumvented somewhat by the ability to "chunk" information. In discussing the number of items that one can hold in immediate memory, Miller noted that the items did not have to be single bits but could be chunks of information. A chunk is defined as any meaningful unit of information.

For example, take about 14 seconds to try memorizing the following sequence of 14 individual letters:

IB MJ FKTW AUS ACD

This is difficult to do because 14 bits exceeds the capacity of your working memory. But what if you rearranged the same letters into meaningful units like these:

IBM JFK TWA USA CD

Now the letters form five chunks that are easy to remember. We see IBM as a single unit, as is 911 or the phrase "a fat cat." Social Security numbers would be much more difficult to remember without the hyphens that group them into three memory-

We need to realize that these limitations can be circumvented somewhat by the ability to "chunk" information.

Being able to see how information fits together in chunks is, therefore, a hallmark of learning, a way of working with larger and larger amounts of information.

manageable chunks. Phone numbers are not remembered as a list of ten numbers but as two chunks of three numbers and one chunk of four. Grouping information together in classes or categories is another method of chunking.

The difference between novices and experts in a field appears to be that experts tend (because of their great deal of experience) to organize information into much bigger chunks while novices work with isolated bits of information. Experienced chess players can reproduce the exact configuration of all 16 chess pieces on a board after examining it for only five seconds. How is this possible? Researchers at the University of Pittsburgh's Learning Research and Development Center estimate that a chess master has stored roughly 100,000 patterns of pieces on the chess board in long-term memory (Chase & Simon, 1973). By using this information, the player can code the position of all 16 pieces in just two or three chunks of information, numbers that can easily be handled by working memory. The manner in which the chess master chunks information together gives us an important clue for "improving" working memory. Although we cannot increase the number of chunks we can store, we can (by reorganizing or recoding) increase the amount of information that can be stored in each chunk.

Being able to see how information fits together in chunks is, therefore, a hallmark of learning, a way of working with larger and larger amounts of information. One of the problems we have when attempting to teach something to another person is that we see connections that the other person does not yet see. We may be tempted to "give" our students the benefit of our experience, and tell them what the connections are, how the information fits together. This seldom works; the students need to make the connections themselves. Mark Twain once said, "If teaching were the same as telling, we'd all be so smart we could hardly stand it." He was right, unfortunately; teaching *isn't* the same as

Mark Twain once said, "If teaching were the same as telling, we'd all be so smart we could hardly stand it."

telling. Teaching is guiding and facilitating the formation of neural connections in the student's brain. Chess players don't become experts by simply having someone telling them how to play. They have to do the work themselves, playing thousands of games, becoming familiar with the patterns, and reorganizing the information to be able to "see" the chunks. Our students are no different. We provide the experience and the guidance, but they have to do the work. So, what does the work look like? Just as working memory's capacity can be increased by chunking, the duration of information also can be increased by working with the information. This process is called rehearsal or practice.

Rote Rehearsal

There are many ways to rehearse information or a skill. One type, called rote rehearsal, consists of repeating the information or the action over and over. It's what we generally use when we need to remember a phone number, from the time we look it up until we dial the phone. It's also what we use to learn to ride a bicycle or to touch-type. Rote rehearsal, however, is much more effective for learning a procedure (a skill or habit) than for remembering a phone number. (If someone says something to you as you are repeating the phone number, it's quickly lost.) It is easy to see why rote rehearsal is essential for forming the strong neural connections necessary to get a skill or habit to the automatic level. Driving a car without paying conscious attention, or decoding text so automatically that you are able to concentrate on the meaning of what you are reading, requires that you practice or rehearse these skills repeatedly. You don't learn to swim or play the piano by reading a book about it. Although the information in a book may be helpful, it is still necessary to practice the skill repeatedly to develop it to the point where it works well without conscious attention. Benjamin Bloom (1986) labeled this

You don't learn to swim or play the piano by reading a book about it.

"automaticity" and described it as the ability to perform a skill unconsciously with speed and accuracy while consciously carrying on other brain functions. He interviewed numerous experts in a variety of fields and reported how they all talked about the great amount of practice and training time they devoted to their work, some as many as 50 hours per week.

Elaborative Rehearsal

Some of what we teach in schools requires students to engage in hours, if not years, of rote rehearsal. Examples are reading (decoding), writing, classroom procedures, and basic arithmetic processes. Much of the standard curriculum, however, falls into the semantic memory category, where rote rehearsal is not as effective a method of practice. Repeatedly rehearsing a dictionary definition (commonly called memorizing) may allow students to write the definition correctly on the test (if no one talks to them just before the test), but as every teacher knows, it may not have any meaning and is seldom remembered a week later. The same is true for *comprehending* an event in history, an algorithm in mathematics, or a formula in chemistry. For these types of learning, elaborative rehearsal strategies are much more effective.

Elaborative rehearsal is a broad category encompassing a variety of strategies. These strategies encourage the learner to elaborate on the information in a manner that enhances understanding and retention of that information. Usually, elaborative strategies increase memory by making the information more meaningful or relevant to the learner. Why does elaborative rehearsal work more effectively than rote rehearsal for these types of data? A look at some of the research on forgetting, and a review of the things we've learned about how the brain processes information, will help us understand.

Usually, elaborative strategies increase memory by making the information more meaningful or relevant to the learner.

Meaning and Retention

The brain is continuously scanning the world to make sense of the constant bombardment of stimuli impinging on the body. This overarching characteristic of human brain functioning is understandable when we recall that the main purpose of a brain is the survival of the individual and of the species. If the brain deemed every stimulus to be important, we would be overloaded to the point of not being able to make decisions essential for our survival. Fortunately, the brain sifts through all incoming sensory stimuli and selects those that are the most relevant or meaningful. The brain's determination of what is meaningful and what is not is reflected not only in the initial perceptual processes but also in the conscious processing of information. Recall that the information storage mechanisms of the brain can be best described as networks of associations. These networks are formed over our lifetimes by the experiences we've had. Information that fits into or adds to an existing network has a much better chance of storage than information that doesn't.

What happens when information has no meaning? Hermann Ebbinghaus conducted one of the first research studies on memory in 1885. He made up long lists of nonsense syllables (*zek, dof, fok,* and so forth) which he then memorized. His purpose in using nonsense syllables was to eliminate any effects his personal experience might have on his ability to recall the syllables. He would memorize a list of syllables by heart well enough that he could recite it two times in a row. He then tested his recall over several days. His measurement of forgetting was the time he needed to relearn the list until he could recall it with no errors. This method produced a predictable curve, which is shown in Figure 6.3. Ebbinghaus's curve shows what happens to retention of material when there are no previous associations or meaning (Ornstein, 1998).

The brain is continuously scanning the world to make sense out of the constant bombardment of stimuli impinging on the body.

Information that fits into or adds to an existing network has a much better chance of storage than information that doesn't.

Brain
Matters: Translating Research into Classroom Practice

In our attempts to help learners store information and improve their ability to recall it, we need to make certain that what we are teaching is not "nonsense" to the student's brain. It is essential that we take advantage of the brain's natural proclivity to attend to what is meaningful.

Making Meaning Using Associations

One of the most effective ways to make information meaningful is to associate or compare the new concept with a known concept, to hook the unfamiliar with something familiar. This is

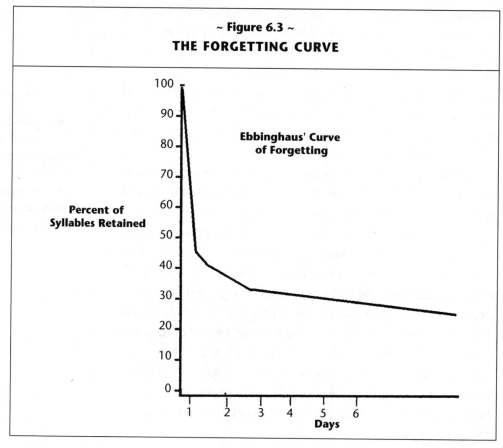

~ Figure 6.3 ~
THE FORGETTING CURVE

Percent of Syllables Retained

Ebbinghaus' Curve of Forgetting

Days

Source: *Psychology: The Study of Human Experience* (2nd ed.), by Robert E. Ornstein, 1998, San Diego, CA: Harcourt Brace Jovanovich, p. 332. Reproduced by permission.

often accomplished using analogies, similes, and sometimes metaphors. In attempting to explain the concept of parallel lines, a teacher would probably point out to the learners that they see them everywhere, railroad tracks, the sides of a sheet of paper and on doors and windows. In doing this, the teacher is forming an association in students' minds between a "foreign" mathematical concept and something they already understand. In the same manner, you could explain how chunking increases the capacity of working memory by using an analogy of a purse that can hold seven pennies, seven dimes, or seven quarters.

If you wanted learners to understand why the brain organizes information into networks, you might ask them to think about looking for a book in a library where the volumes are arranged in a random fashion. Have them estimate how long it would take to find the book. The same is true of the human brain where, if information were not stored in networks or categories, retrieval of information would take forever. In studying fish for the first time, students will have an easier time understanding the function of gills if they have already studied the function of lungs in a mammal and if the teacher points out how they are analogous. The most effective associations link new learning to something that is personally relevant to the student. This is why teachers use wins and losses of soccer games in teaching students to figure percentages, or talk about "math families" when working with younger learners.

Using Associations for Less Meaningful Material

There are some things students need to have "at their fingertips" that have little inherent meaning. When meaning or relevance is difficult to establish (such as remembering the letters of the alphabet or the stages of cell division in mitosis), using a mnemonic device is another effective elaboration technique. Acronyms and acrostics associate a list of items in order with a known word or sentence, thereby making them much easier to

One of the most effective ways to make information meaningful is to associate or compare the new concept with a known concept, to hook the unfamiliar with something familiar.

Our own experience validates that we remember for a longer time events that elicit emotions in us; this idea is also supported by a lot of research.

remember. Anyone who has ever studied music knows that the spaces between the lines on the treble clef spell FACE. We'll look at other examples of mnemonics in Part III of this book.

Emotion and Retention

The neurochemical system that primes the body for emergency also stamps the moment in memory with extra vividness.

In Chapter 5, we saw that emotion strongly influences the determination of whether or not the brain initially pays attention to information. The short path between the thalamus and the amygdala ensures that we react quickly to emotionally relevant information. But that is not the only result of facing potentially dangerous or emotionally laden situations. In addition to the behavioral reaction, the event is nearly always stamped with extra vividness, which results in enhanced memory. Our own experience validates that we remember for a longer time events that elicit emotions in us; this idea is also supported by a lot of research (LeDoux, 1996). To understand why, we need to look at the neurochemical nature of the stress response.

The Stress (Fight-or-Flight) Response

The chemical chain of events of the stress response begins with the perception of an emotionally relevant event. The psychological sentinel of the brain, the amygdala, sends a message via the hypothalamus that engages the entire body and readies it to meet the demands of the situation. Many hormones are involved in carrying out these bodily responses, commonly called the stress response, but three play a major role. First are epinephrine and norepinephrine (also known as adrenalin and noradrenalin), which you read about in Chapter 4. Although these two substances sometimes act as neurotransmitters in the brain, they also circulate as hormones in the bloodstream. Here they act in seconds to set the stress response in motion, affecting the endocrine, circulatory, muscular, and digestive systems.

During the stress response, your heart rate increases, blood pressure goes up, senses become more alert, muscles tense, palms become sweaty, blood-clotting elements increase in the blood-stream, and all centers for movement become mobilized. Simultaneously, cortical memory systems retrieve any knowledge relevant to the emergency at hand, taking precedence over other strands of thought. Stress does not heighten or increase all systems, however; some actually are curbed. The digestive and immune systems are suppressed during the stress response because they are not essential at the moment. Whereas epinephrine and norepinephrine act in seconds, a third hormone, cortisol, which is secreted by the adrenal glands, backs up the activity of the stress response for minutes or hours. Cortisol, as we will see later, can have negative effects. But first, let's look at the positive effects of these hormones.

Educators need to recognize the power of emotion to increase retention, and plan classroom instruction accordingly.

The Stress Response and Memory

This response system obviously is critical for survival; it can save your life. But what does it have to do with memory? The neurochemical system that primes the body for emergency also stamps the moment in memory with extra vividness. Here's how neuroscientists explain this phenomenon. Epinephrine and norepinephrine, which are secreted by the adrenal cortex to activate the automatic responses we have been discussing, find their way back up to the temporal lobe of the brain. The action of these hormones in this area enhances memory for the event that activated the stress response. Studies by Jim McGaugh and his colleagues at the University of California (UC) at Irvine showed that giving an injection of epinephrine to rats right after they have learned something enhances their memory of the learning situation (LeDoux, 1996). Another researcher at UC Irvine, Larry Cahill, has demonstrated the same effect in humans, using epinephrine a little differently but producing a similar effect. Under

Solving real-life problems is another way to raise the emotional and motivational stakes.

normal circumstances, subjects show enhanced memory for emotional pictures over neutral ones. When Cahill gives his subjects a drug that blocks epinephrine soon after viewing an emotionally laden picture, their recall of the emotional pictures is decreased, and they do not remember them any better than neutral ones (Cahill, 2000). In his book *The Emotional Brain*, Joseph LeDoux says the following about this type of research:

> This suggests that if adrenaline [epinephrine] is released naturally (from the adrenal gland) in some situation, that experience will be remembered especially well. Since emotional arousal usually results in the release of adrenaline, it might be expected . . . that explicit conscious memory of emotional situations would be stronger than the explicit memory of nonemotional situations (1996, p. 206).

Cahill (2000) believes that anything you do that engages students' emotional and motivational interest will quite naturally involve this system and result in stronger memories of that which engaged the attention. He states that although investigators have conducted most of the research in this area in the area of fear, it also holds true for even mildly emotional or positive events. For example, the mechanism should be just as involved when you learned you had won the lottery as when you heard of the explosion of the space shuttle *Challenger*. However, the more intense the arousal, the stronger the imprint. It is almost as if the brain has two memory systems: one for ordinary facts and one for those that are emotionally charged.

Adding an Emotional Hook to Learning

Educators need to recognize the power of emotion to increase retention, and plan classroom instruction accordingly. Activities such as simulations and role plays are often highly engaging and enhance not only the meaning of the material but also the emotional connections. Teachers who have their students act out a particular event of history or form a mathematical equation using fellow students are increasing the chances of retention of the event or the equation. As simple an activity as setting up a grocery store in the classroom, to learn about the value of coins and bills and how to figure change, is certainly more likely to hook into the emotional/motivational network than completing a worksheet on the same subject.

Solving real-life problems is another way to raise the emotional and motivational stakes. For example, students in one school district acquire problems from local businesses and work out solutions, which they then present to the owners. They have received high praise for their achievements, and I doubt that the students will ever forget the experience. In another experience likely to stay in students' long-term memory, a group of middle school students designed a way to save water in their state, contacted their state legislator to help them draft a bill, then lobbied for passage of the bill in the state capital. Effective teachers, without knowing the neurological basis of the effect emotion has on learning, often intuitively design ways to make what students are studying more meaningful and emotional. They do this by bringing in parents as guest speakers, taking students on field trips, holding mock trials or debates on historical or current events, designing experiments so students "discover" the process, having students build models or take notes by mind mapping, and countless other activities. Think back on your own school experiences: Which ones stand out? Chances are you'll be able to recall the emotional component of those experiences that caused you to remember them over all others.

Effective teachers, without knowing the neurological basis of the effect emotion has on learning, often design ways to make what students are studying more meaningful and emotional.

The ability to experience and talk about our emotions is a singularly wonderful human quality, but it has its downside.

The Flip Side of Emotion

If you have no stress in your life, you probably won't get out of bed in the morning; if you have too much stress in your life, chances are you won't get out of bed in the morning. As with many things in life, more is not necessarily better, especially when it comes to the stress response. The ability to experience and talk about our emotions is a singularly wonderful human quality, but it has its downside. The stress response was designed for life in caves, but we don't live there anymore. The contemporary human brain doesn't distinguish between actual physical danger and psychological danger; it sets the same physiological chain of events in motion in either case. Having your blood pressure go up, blood clotting elements released into your bloodstream, and your immune system suppressed is fine if you are faced with a cave bear. But it isn't particularly helpful when someone pulls into a parking space you thought was yours. The stress response, with its release of cortisol and epinephrine, was designed to last a relatively short time, until you outran the bear or became its dinner. In contemporary life, however, we often extend the response by talking about the stressful event, reliving it, or worrying that it will happen again. We have a tendency to keep ourselves in a chronic, prolonged fight-or-flight state, with potentially negative consequences. High concentrations of cortisol over a long period of time can provoke hippocampal deterioration and cognitive decline. With prolonged stress, the immune system is compromised, increasing the risk of illness, acceleration of disease, and retardation of growth (Sapolsky, 1994).

Obviously students can and do suffer the same stress-related disorders as adults. But in the classroom, a student can perceive even a mild stressor to be threatening, initiating the stress response and lessening the student's ability to perform. You will probably have no difficulty enumerating some circumstances

We have a tendency to keep ourselves in a chronic, prolonged fight-or-flight state, with potentially negative consequences.

during which this can happen: being bullied or laughed at, taking part in timed testing, being called on when not prepared, or general fear of failure. Under these conditions, emotion is dominant over cognition; and the rational/thinking cortex is less efficient. (Have you ever received an insult and not been able to think of a retort until the next day?)

Emotion is a double-edged sword, with the ability to enhance learning or impede it. Educators need to understand the biological underpinnings of emotion to provide emotionally healthy and exciting school environments that promote optimal learning.

Emotion is a double-edged sword, with the ability to enhance learning or impede it.

Synapse Strengtheners

1. Using the information processing model diagram, explain to a colleague the major differences between sensory memory and working memory.

2. Without looking back at the book, write a paragraph about the difference between rote and elaborative rehearsal, giving examples of appropriate uses of each in the classroom.

3. If you are reading this book as part of a study group, ask members of the group to select a topic or unit that they normally teach in a traditional, didactic manner. Design a way to make it more meaningful to the students. Share these plans with the group.

4. Design a lesson to teach your students about the emotional nature of their brains and why emotion can be a double-edged sword.

7 | Long-Term Memory: The Brain's Storage System

The capacity of our long-term memories is unknown but is considered to be extremely large— by some estimates containing a million billion connections.

You smell a particular antiseptic, and the memory of a hospital stay comes flooding into your consciousness, even though you haven't thought about that event for years. At a high school reunion, the sight of a former classmate who was in your chemistry class brings back a memory that you didn't know was there. At a party, people start singing songs from the 1960s and you remember most of the words to songs you haven't sung for 30 years. You haven't ridden a bicycle for years, but when your nephew asks if you can ride, you climb on his new bicycle and soon are showing him how to perform a "wheelie." You ask yourself, "How did that happen?" You can thank your long-term memory for these memories you are able to hold onto from minutes to decades. Without it, you would be unable to learn or profit from experience. Life would be a moment-to-moment occurrence, similar to that experienced by H. M., as described in Chapter 2.

Long-term memory, the last part of our information-processing model, is truly remarkable in what it allows us to recall. When we compare long-term memory to sensory or working memory (both of which are relatively short-term), we find that it is just what its name implies, long term. The information stored in long-term memory is relatively permanent but not always accurate. The capacity of our long-term memories is unknown but is considered to be extremely large—by some estimates containing a million billion connections. In this chapter we will look at the processes that allow our brain to store and retrieve information over time and the factors that influence the strength of these memories. It is a fascinating journey into the unconscious depths of human memory and one that has powerful implications for teaching and learning.

Types of Memory Storage

Figure 7.1 shows several subheadings in the "long-term memory" box. While we often think of memory as a single process, memory storage is actually more than one type of process. As early as 1911, the French philosopher Henri Bergson stated that our past survives in two fundamentally different forms, conscious and unconscious (Schacter, 1996). Scientists usually characterize these two forms (and their subcategories) as procedural or declarative. As we will see, these two forms of memory are localized in different neural systems.

Procedural Memory—Skills and Priming

Procedural memory is knowing *how* versus knowing *what.* It is sometimes called *nondeclarative:* You do not need to "declare" anything, and you may not be able to say much about what you are doing, for the information to be stored. The first type of procedural memory is your ability to store automatic processes for routine actions. You can think of these processes as skills, the "how" to do things. They may be simple procedures, such as walking, brushing your teeth, or tying your shoes, or they may be more complex, such as driving a car or decoding words. These procedures have in common their automatic nature. After a good deal of repetition and practice, we perform them without conscious thought. The famous cognitive psychologist Jerome Bruner called procedural memory a *memory without record* (Squire & Kandel, 2000). The automatic procedures form a sort of unconscious stimulus-response bond. Once we have a skill or habit at this level, however, it becomes difficult to access it in any way except by performing it. Imagine trying to teach someone to tie a shoe, swing a golf club, or write a word without physically demonstrating it. We no longer know how we accomplish the procedure. Its separate parts or its rules of operation are virtually inaccessible to our consciousness.

Procedural memory is knowing how versus knowing what.

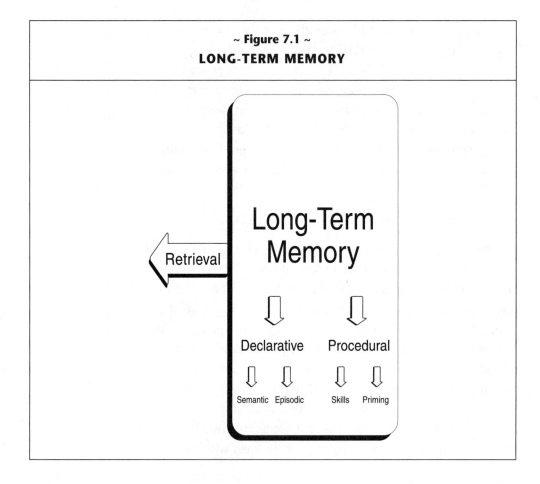

~ Figure 7.1 ~
LONG-TERM MEMORY

Most of the skills we have been discussing involve motor activity, but some types of skillful behavior are not based on learned movements. An example of a nonmotor skill is reading. When you first learn to read, your eyes move slowly from word to word; but with a great deal of practice, you move through the words much more quickly. Skilled readers move their eyes about four times a second, taking in the meaning of more than 300 words a minute (Squire & Kandel, 2000).

A second type of procedural memory is known as *priming*. Priming involves being influenced by a past experience without any awareness of consciously remembering that experience. In a sense, priming is similar to the skill learning mentioned in the previous section. In neither case are you consciously aware of what you are doing—which is why both skills and priming are sometimes called *implicit* memory, in contrast to conscious recollection, or *explicit* memory (Schacter, 1996). In priming experiments, researchers show subjects lists of words, then hours or days later show them another list and ask whether they have seen any of the words before. On a second task, subjects are given the beginning of a word from the lists (abs___ for absent and inc___ for income) and asked to complete the word. The subjects perform much better on the fragmentation completion task (nondeclarative or implicit memory) than on the task in which they have to identify whether or not they have seen the word before (declarative or explicit memory). It may be that for a period of time after seeing a word, less neural activity is required to process that word again (Squire & Kandel, 2000). This has been seen in amnesiacs who are able to learn new procedural skills but have no memory of learning them. This is why H. M. is able to improve his performance of new motor skills (such as mirror writing), but does not remember ever having done them before (Amaral, 2000). This type of experiment indicates that our memory can be influenced by experiences that we fail to recollect con-

Having seen or experienced something more than once seems to prime our ability to recall it later.

sciously. Having seen or experienced something previously seems to prime our ability to recall it later. Procedural memory, whether skill learning or priming, provides dramatic evidence that unconscious mental activities do exist.

Declarative Memory—Semantic and Episodic Recall

Declarative memory is our ability to store and recall information that we can declare (speak or write). Unlike procedural memory, declarative memory requires conscious processing; it is reflective rather than reflexive. Instead of the automatic, unconscious recall of how to do something, declarative memory permits us to consciously recall and discuss what something is, or recall and describe an event that occurred in the past. This dual function has led to declarative memory being subdivided into two categories, *episodic* and *semantic memory*.

Episodic memory is sometimes called "source memory," because it involves remembering where and when information was acquired. It allows you to recall a hike you once took, how much you loved your 1st grade teacher, and a surprise party on your 16th birthday. It is your record of faces, music, facts, and your individual experiences, a sort of "autobiographical reference" (Squire & Kandel, 2000). As critical as episodic memory is (it's important to remember where you parked your car), it can at times be problematic. The brain does not store memories in a linear manner, as a tape recorder or video camera does; it stores memories in neural circuits or networks. When we recall an event, we are actually reconstructing it. While many events are important or emotional enough to be remembered, the details often escape us. What the brain does in this case is "fill in" the details. This process is called *refabrication*; it can be defined as the reconstructing of a memory from bits and pieces of truth. As we tell our stories over and over, we embellish them, add to them, and make them a bit more elaborate. Eventually the refabrication

The brain does not store memories in a linear manner, as a tape recorder or video camera does; it stores memories in neural circuits or networks.

becomes the memory, and it is virtually impossible to distinguish it from what actually happened. Even though the memory of the event is quite vivid, the details may actually be inaccurate.

Semantic memory, on the other hand, is generally fairly accurate. Semantic memory includes words, the symbols for them, the rules for manipulating the words, and their meanings. It also consists of rules of grammar, chemical formulas, rules of computing in mathematics, and your general knowledge about your world. These facts are normally independent of a particular time or place. Knowing that $6 + 7 = 42$ is an example of semantic memory; remembering what grade you were in when you learned the multiplication tables is an illustration of episodic memory.

The Cellular Basis of Memory

We have been looking at the big picture of memory and its various types. It is important to remember, however, that underlying our memory (no matter which type) are changes in the neurons and connections between neurons that form the physiological basis of storing and retrieving information. What are the cellular mechanisms that allow information to make the crucial leap from working memory to long-term memory? Endel Tulving, considered by some to be the world's foremost authority on cognitive theories of memory, states:

> As a scientist I am compelled to the conclusion—not postulation, not assumption, but conclusion—that there must exist certain physical-chemical changes in the nervous tissue that correspond to the storage of information, or to the engram, changes that constitute the necessary conditions of remembering (Tulving, cited in Gazzaniga,1997, p. 97).

The study of the molecular events underlying memory formation is one of the most exciting fields of neuroscientific study.

The study of the molecular events underlying memory formation is one of the most exciting fields of neuroscientific study. The introduction to memory in Chapter 5 mentions "Hebb's Law." In the 1940s, Canadian neuroscientist Donald Hebb proposed that a synapse between two neurons is strengthened if the neurons are active or firing at the same time. His theory is generally accepted in the field of neuroscience today; however, *how* this occurs is still open to some debate (Squire & Kandel, 2000). One current hypothesis is that the synapses between neurons representing experiences become strengthened or potentiated over a period of time. This is referred to as *long-term potentiation* (LTP). LTP has been demonstrated in the laboratory with animals and has been the predominant model of the cellular basis of memory for more than two decades. Not all neuroscientists agree that the experiments necessarily reflect what happens during the storage of a memory in humans, but most agree that it is at least one of the important mechanisms involved in changing the synaptic strength between neurons in neural networks.

One current hypothesis is that the synapse between neurons representing experiences becomes strengthened or potentiated over a period of time.

Long-Term Potentiation (LTP)

How might LTP result in a memory? First, let's review what we understand about how neurons allow us to see or to hear. We know that the experience of seeing a yellow rose or a blue ball is the result of the activation of a particular group of neurons in the visual cortex. Likewise, a group of neurons firing together in the auditory cortex will result in the experience of a certain tone or note of music. A memory appears to entail a similar firing of neurons, but the pattern of firing remains encoded in a neural circuit or network after the stimulation that originally caused the neurons to fire has ceased. You can remember the image of the rose or the ball, and you can hear the melody of the song in your head. It appears that this is possible because when two or more neurons are active at the same time, they become more sensitive, i.e., more likely to fire a second time. The more often the pattern of neurons is activated, the more efficient the synapse becomes. This increased efficacy of the synapses is what many scientists refer to as LTP. Researchers have demonstrated LTP in several parts of the hippocampus and surrounding structures in the medial temporal lobe, which we will see are critical to the formation and storage of memories.

There is some evidence that the chemicals released at the synapse that lead to LTP may result in the modification of proteins, synthesis of new proteins (implicated in memory), and changes in gene transcription (Amaral & Soltesz, 1997).

Growth of Synapses

In the 1960s, Marian Diamond, Mark Rosenzweig, and their colleagues at the University of California, Berkeley, demonstrated that substantial changes in the brain's architecture can be influenced by an animal's environment (Diamond, 1988). Somewhat later, William Greenough at the University of Illinois extended the research on "enriched" environments. Enrichment for the rats in both these studies was provided by placing a colony of rats together in a large cage with toys that were changed every few days. The rats raised in the enriched environment showed growth in the thickness and weight of their cortices, due to larger cortical neurons, heavier branching of dendrites, and larger synapses. Increases of up to 20 percent more synapses per neuron were found in the visual cortex of some of the animals. These structural changes in the rats' brains resulted in their being better able to solve complex maze problems. [Diamond reports that wild rats obtained from their natural environment had even more dendritic growth—and heavier cortices—than those in enriched environments (M. C. Diamond, personal communication, July 2000).]

There is still much to be understood before the mystery of how experiences are stored at a cellular level comes close to being

The more often the pattern of neurons is activated, the more efficient the synapse becomes.

Truly amazing changes take place in the neural connections in our brains, and the methods we use to structure learning experiences for our students affect the strength and duration of those changes.

solved. Whatever the process or processes may turn out to be, the fact remains that when we learn, truly amazing changes take place in the neural connections in our brains, and the methods we use to structure learning experiences for our students affect the strength and duration of those changes.

How Are Memories Stored?

Suppose you were asked to recall an event in your life, perhaps a graduation celebration or a surprise birthday party. In all probability you would be able to describe many aspects of that experience: the people who were there, the food that was served, the room you were in, the sound of people singing "Happy Birthday," and perhaps some of the gifts you received. The memory probably came to you in a fairly complete form, so that it seems that this particular memory must be stored in a special place in your brain, ready to be recalled in its entirety whenever you wish. But in actuality, no complete scenarios or pictures are stored anywhere in the brain; you have to reconstruct these memories every time. While this may seem inefficient and even counter-intuitive, the process by which we encode experience and later recall it really makes a lot of sense.

In his book *Inside the Brain*, science writer Ronald Kotulak uses the metaphor of eating a meal to represent the encoding and storing of information:

The brain gobbles up its external environment in bites and chunks through its sensory system: vision, hearing, smell, touch, and taste. Then the digested world is reassembled in the form of trillions of connections between brain cells that are constantly growing or dying, or becoming stronger or weaker, depending upon the richness of the banquet (Kotulak, 1996, p. 4).

When you think carefully about it, this is efficient. Our experiences are disassembled into parts and stored in specialized networks of cells. The same brain cells can be used many times to recall similar lines or colors or smells. For example, the cells in the visual cortex that allow us to perceive the color red can be used to see a red rose, a red heart, the red in a sunset, or a red tie. The same is true in the auditory cortex and other sensory areas as well. In a sense, many parts of the brain each contribute something different to the memory of a single event. Our knowledge is built on bits and pieces of many aspects of a given thing—its shape, color, taste, or movement. But these aspects are not laid down in a single place; there is no memory center in the brain that represents an entire event at a single location.

The same brain cells can be used many times to recall similar lines or colors or smells.

How Are Memories Recalled?

If memories are not stored in specific locations in the brain, how do we retrieve them? Our ability to remember is essentially a process of reconstruction or reactivation. As we have seen, the various elements of past experience reside all over the brain—in the visual cortex, auditory cortex, and other areas. Antonio Damasio (1994), professor and head of the department of neurology at the University of Iowa College of Medicine, describes *recall* as an activation of all these separate sites in unison, creating an integrated experience. You don't even need all the pieces to reconstruct the total, just the definitive elements. Recall the picture of the dalmatian (Figure 5.3) in Chapter 5. The dog is not clearly defined, but you don't need all the components to reconstruct the total picture, just the definitive elements. When a critical mass of sensory neurons is activated, the brain fills in the missing portions to complete the picture. Keep in mind, though, that the image of the dalmatian must have been previously stored in order to be retrieved; that is, if you had never before seen a dalmatian, you probably wouldn't be able to fill in the blanks.

The same is true when remembering an event. Depending on the cue or reminder, only certain fragments of the total memory may be activated. If the cue is weak or unclear, what is reactivated may differ from the original memory or even belong to another episode. This is why episodic memory details are often fuzzy or even completely inaccurate, and why "eye-witnesses" of events are generally unreliable. Memory researchers Elizabeth and Geoffrey Loftus are well-known for their studies of how memories can be modified or distorted by the type of questions asked in a memory retrieval test. They have also demonstrated that false memories can be planted if the memories contain some aspect that reasonably could have occurred (Loftus & Loftus, 1975).

Brain Structures Involved in Storage and Retrieval

Declarative and procedural memory, while sharing many of the same cellular mechanisms, do not employ the same brain structures for their processing. The two major structures involved in memory processing are the cortex and a part of the brain called the medial temporal lobe. It appears that the brain stores memories in the same structures that are engaged in initially perceiving and processing stimuli; however, these structures differ, depending on whether the memory is procedural or declarative. Understanding the anatomy involved in these two types of memory will further clarify the types of activities and practice best suited to each one.

The Procedural Pathway to Long-Term Storage

You may drive your car on a familiar route, arrive at your destination, and realize that you were not aware of driving there.

When you meet someone new, you automatically extend your hand in greeting. You may read a page of text, get to the bottom of the page, and realize that you do not remember what you just read, usually because you were thinking about something other than the text. These motor skills, habits, and perceptual skills are all examples of procedural or non-declarative memory, and all were accomplished without your conscious awareness. As mentioned earlier, trying to consciously express any of these skills while performing them impairs your performance. But if you think back to when you first learned to drive or to read, none of these skills or habits were automatic. They required a great deal of conscious attention and practice.

In the early stage of skill (procedural) learning, three brain areas are involved in laying down the new pathways: the prefrontal cortex, the parietal cortex, and the cerebellum. Their combined activity allows you to pay the necessary conscious attention to the task and ensures that the correct movements are assembled correctly. After practice, however, all these areas show less activity, and other structures, including the motor cortex, become more engaged (Squire & Kandel, 2000).

In nonmotor procedural learning, such as decoding words, the brain area that appears to be most heavily involved is the visual cortex. With extended practice, we improve our ability to discriminate between different line orientations and letter configurations. The ultimate long-term effect is to change the actual neural structure of the visual cortex, which alters the machinery of perception over time. Remember that these changes do not involve understanding word meanings, only the ability to recognize the configurations more quickly. All this occurs outside awareness, as has been demonstrated by amnesiac patients who are able, with practice, to improve their speed in reading a selection of prose, but who do not remember the text in any ordinary sense (Squire & Kandel, 2000).

The ultimate long-term effect is to change the actual neural structure of the visual cortex, which alters the machinery of perception over time.

The Declarative Memory Pathway to Long-Term Storage

The journey from perception to storage of both semantic and episodic memory begins with the sensory receptors receiving stimuli. The stimuli register in the appropriate areas of the cortex (visual, auditory, etc.) and then travel to the hippocampus and an adjacent cluster of structures within the medial temporal lobe. These structures register the stimuli as neural patterns in much the same way as they were registered in the cortex. Note that the hippocampus is not the ultimate storage repository of memory; rather, it acts as an intermediate storage site for cortical representations on their way to long-term memory (Squire & Kandel, 2000). These representations can be reactivated during recall, and each time they are replayed the messages are sent back to the cortex, where the stimuli originally registered. This reactivation of the original neural patterns strengthens them, making them less likely to fade. With repeated activation, the memories form neural links that become more or less permanently embedded in the frontal cortex and temporal cortex. These links remain in long-term memory long after the hippocampal representations have faded. So we can see why the hippocampus is essential for forming new memories, but it becomes less essential over time as these memories are eventually stored in the cortex. This provides an explanation of why amnesiacs with damage to the hippocampus can no longer lay down new permanent memories, but often are able to remember long-ago events that occurred before the brain damage.

Consolidation

Patients receiving electroconvulsive therapy (a controlled series of electric shocks to the brain) often forget experiences and learnings that occurred just before the treatment. This condition is called *retrograde amnesia*. However, if the treatment is delayed for a period of time after learning new information, the shock is less likely to disrupt recall. The reason for this appears to be that even after an event has been placed into memory, some time must pass for the memory trace to become fully established or organized in the brain.

In the late 19th century, German psychologists Georg Müller and Alfons Pilzecher conducted studies using the nonsense syllables of Ebbinghaus's experiments and found that learning a second list of syllables immediately after learning a first list interfered with later recall of the first list. Without disruption, the newly formed memories gradually became more stable. The researchers labeled this gelling or setting time the *consolidation period* (Squire & Kandel, 2000). We now know that memory is not formed at the moment information is acquired; memory is not a simple fixation process. Rather, it is dynamic, with unconscious processes (called consolidation) that continue to strengthen and stabilize the connections over days, weeks, months, and years (Gazzaniga, Ivry, & Mangun, 1998). Consolidation is undoubtedly enhanced by rehearsal. When we "replay" our experiences (talk and think about them), we are providing more opportunities for consolidation. Perhaps this is why instruction that allows students to hook new information to previous experiences increases the strength and complexity of their neural connections and, therefore, the retention of the information.

Scientists have studied the consolidation process extensively in rats, mice, and fruit flies. One interesting set of experiments suggests that consolidation requires new protein synthesis. When mice receive an injection of a substance that inhibits protein synthesis just before training, they have a profound loss of long-term memory when tested three or more hours later. Mice given a saline injection show no long-term memory loss.

The researchers labeled this gelling or setting time the consolidation period.

Instruction that allows students to hook new information to previous experiences increases the strength and complexity of their neural connections and, therefore, the retention of the information.

Brain
Matters: Translating Research into Classroom Practice

Consolidation seems to be the result of biological changes underlying the retention of learned information. What are these biological changes? Given what we know about the importance of the hippocampus in the formation of long-term memory, it is not surprising that the function of the hippocampus, and of nearby structures in the medial temporal lobe, is integral to consolidation. Without the mediating effects of the hippocampus, consolidation could not take place. As we practice or repeat our experiences, however, they may become consolidated and the hippocampal structures will no longer be needed.

Consolidation seems to be the result of biological changes underlying the retention of learned information.

Sleep and Consolidation

Recent research also points to sleep as another player in the consolidation process. During sleep, particularly during the rapid eye movement (REM) stage, our brains are relieved from processing the continual input of information that occurs during waking. In his book *Searching for Memory*, Daniel Schacter tells of a hypothesis developed by neuroscientist Jonathan Winson, who suggested that during sleep, the brain continues to work through the experiences of the day. Winson's ideas have recently received support from research on animal brains. Recordings taken of rats' brains during sleep indicate that the hippocampus is particularly active "playing back" recent experiences to the cortex, where they will eventually be stored (Schacter, 1996). You have probably noticed that your own dreams often contain fragments of what you did during the day. It may be that your brain is replaying these experiences, helping to consolidate them just as consciously reviewing information during waking hours does. If this is true, sleep is an important participant in the formation of long-term memories.

Consolidation in Motor Memory

Researchers most frequently discuss the concept of consolidation in terms of declarative memory, which relies on brain structures in the medial temporal lobe. Recent research indicates that learning motor skills (a procedural memory) also involves consolidation. Researchers at the Massachusetts Institute of Technology Department of Brain and Cognitive Sciences have discovered that "learning a motor skill sets in motion neural processes that continue to evolve after practice has ended" (Brashers-Krug, Shadmehr, & Bizzi, 1996). When subjects learned a second motor task immediately after a first skill was learned, the consolidation of the first motor skill was disrupted. This disruption did not occur if four hours elapsed between learning the first and second skills. The researchers propose that motor skill consolidation relies on the same structures in the medial temporal lobe that are necessary for the consolidation of explicit (declarative) memory tasks.

"Learning a motor skill sets in motion neural processes that continue to evolve after practice has ended."

Educational Implications of Consolidation

It is tempting to try to directly apply the research on consolidation to the classroom. It would be helpful for teachers to know just how long students' brains need to consolidate a particular learning before moving on to another. Unfortunately, the research doesn't give us this kind of detailed information. We do know, however, that consolidation occurs and that it takes time. We also know that teaching something new too soon disrupts consolidation of previous learning. What we don't know is how *much* time is needed for consolidation; and, therefore, we should be wary of specifying time lengths between introduction of concepts or skills. Neuroscience seldom gives us information that can be applied directly to classroom practice, but we need to take what we *know* about consolidation into account when designing instruction. For example, building elaborative rehearsal strategies into our instruction—allowing students time to process information more in depth—may increase the strength of the learning because these strategies allow consolidation to take place.

Teaching for Long-Term Memory

Most learning in life is incidental. In everyday life, generally, we make no particular effort to record our experiences for later. Our interests, preferences, and survival needs direct our attention and determine how well information is encoded. Although incidental learning has value, we cannot trust that everything we need to remember will be "incidentally" encoded. More often than not, we have to expend some effort to make certain that we'll be able to recall the information when we need it. No one knows more about how difficult this can be than teachers. Students often memorize the information for a test and then promptly forget it. The problem is exacerbated by the demands to cover more curriculum—and *covering* is often all that happens. Coverage (going over information superficially) does not build strong neural connections and, therefore, is seldom remembered or remembered incorrectly. This problem is difficult to solve, but perhaps the information in this chapter will help educators understand what is necessary to produce long-term retention of information.

The term *elaborative rehearsal* was introduced in Chapter 6. We are now in a better position to understand why this type of practice is more effective for producing long-term declarative memory than rote rehearsal. The more fully we process information over time, the more connections we make, the more consolidation takes place, and the better the memory will be. In the

The more fully we process information over time, the more connections we make, the more consolidation takes place, and the better the memory will be.

remaining chapters of this book, we discuss a number of elaborative rehearsal strategies. Most of them require students to reflect on the information being taught, relate it to something they already know, form meaningful mental associations, or employ some other effective elaborative encoding strategy.

Synapse Strengtheners

1. Based on the information in this chapter about what is necessary for information to be stored in long-term memory, explain why many educators say, "We need to teach a lot less a lot better."

2. Without looking back at the text, draw a diagram of long-term memory with all its subdivisions. Under each subdivision, write at least one example typical of that type.

3. If you are reading this book as part of a study group, devote one session to discussing what constitutes an enriched environment for students. You might also want to describe the elements of an enriched environment for teachers.

4. Explain to a fellow educator what is meant by consolidation and why it is not a good idea to teach two separate skills close together.

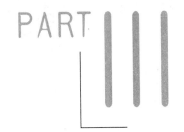

Matching Instruction to How the Brain Learns Best

The most powerful strategies increase retention, understanding, and *students' abilities to apply the concepts they are learning.*

In this final section of the book, we move from looking at the structure and function of the brain and its memory processes to a discussion of how this knowledge might be applied in educational settings. Some material comes from studies conducted by educational researchers and cognitive psychologists, but I have selected many of the strategies and activities because I believe they take advantage of what we're learning about how the brain processes and stores information.

In this respect, much of Part III has its basis in the wisdom of practice more than in research. I believe that one of the best "laboratories" for educational research is the classroom, where creative teachers work to make the curriculum meaningful, try new methods, monitor and adjust their instruction, and share what they have found to be effective. This section of the book includes strategies that I have observed or that teachers of all grade levels and subject areas. have shared with me. I have attempted to provide a "brain-based" rationale for why these strategies work, but I want to make it clear that the rationale is mostly my own, not that of the researchers.

This book addresses curriculum primarily in terms of its relevance or meaning to the students. Not addressed, but vitally important, is how schools and teachers select and structure the curriculum. Of course, we need to be aware of the research on brain structure and function and, as well, try to use this information to teach in meaningful ways so that students truly understand the content. But all this new knowledge will be to no avail if the curriculum is either irrelevant or taught out of context. Pedagogy does not stand alone; it goes hand in hand with intelligently selected content that is structured within meaningful contexts. We need to ask ourselves questions such as, "What are the big ideas or concepts of this lesson?" and "What is the lifelong benefit of what I'm teaching? How will the students be able to use what they are learning today in their adult lives?"

Historically, we have taught subject matter in separate modules—in time blocks at the elementary level or in specialized classes at the secondary level. In recent years, educators have tried to integrate various aspects of the curriculum into more meaningful units. Thematic teaching has become popular in many schools; however, in many instances the thematic units, such as dinosaurs or the rain forest, appear to have been designed with no apparent underlying concepts in mind. It is often difficult to determine why the theme was chosen, let alone answer questions concerning the relevance or application of what teachers are teaching. In her book *Science Continuum of Concepts for Grades K–6*, Karen Olsen writes:

> From brain research, we . . . have come to understand that the brain is a pattern-seeking device in search of meaning and that learning is the acquisition of mental programs for using what we understand. Thus, the most usable and useful curriculum for classroom teachers would be one that made clear for teacher and student what the patterns are (The Concepts to Be Learned) and how those understandings would be used in the real world (Expected Student Performances) (Olsen, 1995, p. 5).

Part III provides examples of activities that match how the brain learns best. Teachers need to consciously select strategies to assist students in learning broad concepts that are embedded within rigorous, relevant content. The strategies and activities in this section serve several different purposes.

First, some strategies assist students in recalling important information. For example, how do we remember how many days are in each month? We use a mnemonic strategy—either a rhyme ("30 days hath September") or we count the peaks and valleys of our knuckles. There's nothing particularly emotional or meaningful in this strategy, but it is certainly useful. Mnemonic strategies have sometimes been denigrated as nothing more than memorizing. At times, however, we need to have relatively meaningless information (such as the spelling of a word, or when to use certain punctuation) at our fingertips. At these times, mnemonic

strategies work very well and need to be in the teacher's repertoire. Research on mnemonic strategies used with special education students has shown that the students may become very
proficient in using the mnemonic as taught, but seldom transfer
the strategy to another area unless taught to do so (Pressley &
Levin, 1978).

A second group of strategies not only helps students remember facts but also assists their understanding of concepts. When
students use manipulatives in math or science (or any other curricular area), they are much more likely to understand the concepts than if they merely read about them. Simulations that take
advantage of the mind-body connection are powerful tools for
retention *and* understanding. For example, the concept of a food
chain or web may be difficult for students to comprehend. But if
the teacher engages students in a simulation where some
"become" different parts of the web and others "become" factors
that influence the web, both retention of individual facts and
understanding of the overall concept will be increased.

Third, the most powerful strategies increase retention, understanding, *and* students' abilities to apply the concepts they are
learning. Nearly any strategy in the second group can fit into this
category if the teacher includes explicit examples of application
and then has students generate examples of when and how a
concept might be used or applied in another area. For example,
the teacher who asks her students to engage in a simulation of
food availability in first-, second-, and third-world countries
could easily follow the exercise with a discussion of how what
they have learned applies to their own lives and of possible solutions to the problem of world hunger.

Making Curriculum Meaningful Through Problems, Projects, and Simulations

8

Learning is a process of building neural networks. Over a lifetime, you have constructed networks in the cortex of your brain containing information about an unbelievable variety of concepts. For example, picture a network that contains information about animals. If you were asked to list everything you know about animals, you would discover you have a tremendous amount of stored knowledge: the difference between a mammal and a reptile, where animals live and what they eat, which animals are kept as pets and which ones are raised primarily for food, which animals are extinct, and even perhaps some information about the cloning of animals in recent years. How was this network formed? In all probability, your brain formed it in three different ways: through concrete experience, representational or symbolic learning, and abstract learning.

Learning is a process of building neural networks.

Three Levels of Learning

Concrete Experience

Imagine that you are a young child going for a walk with your father. Suddenly a small, furry, four-legged creature that you have never seen comes out of a yard and sits on the sidewalk in front of you. After telling you not to be afraid, your father labels this creature for you. He tells you that this is an *animal*, and it is called a *dog*. If he decides that it is a friendly dog, your father may even let you touch it. This experience will be stored in your brain in an actual physiological connection between neurons. If on subsequent walks you encounter this same dog again, the connection will be strengthened, and we say that you have learned what this animal is.

But learning isn't this simple, because there is not just one dog but many dogs in your neighborhood. It won't take long for you to realize that dogs come in many shapes, sizes, and colors. All this information will be incorporated into your "dog network." Some dogs you encounter will be friendly, others will not, and you will add emotional associations to the existing information. This network is well underway to becoming complex, when something puzzling occurs. You are again out for a walk with your father when you encounter another small, furry, four-legged creature. This time you don't need anyone to label it for you. You point to the animal and say, "Dog." Your father laughs and tells you that this animal is not a dog, it's a *cat*. Your brain now has to begin forming a new network containing information about cats. In the course of time, this new web will probably be part of a larger network labeled "animal."

With repeated experiences, your animal network will become stronger, even though it is limited to only two types of animals. Then your parents decide to take you to the zoo. You are now exposed to a large number of creatures you haven't seen before. Some have long necks, others have horns on the ends of their noses, and still others look like cats but are much, much larger. Yet your parents tell you that they are all animals. Amazingly, your brain takes all this information and begins to fit it into the previously established animal network. Because connections in the brain become stronger the more easily they are activated, your dog and cat connections are probably more easily accessed than those for giraffe or tiger. Is there any way these connections can become stronger without daily trips to the zoo?

Representational or Symbolic Learning

Although our brains make some of our strongest links through concrete experience, we are fortunately not limited to learning solely in this way. Continuing the animal example cited before, children enhance their ability to recognize and label zoo animals by looking at the pictures in an animal book that the parents read to them. Children quickly learn to match the name of the animal to its picture. Repeated exposure to the pictures in the book can make the more exotic animals as familiar as domestic pets. But the initial concrete experience (seeing these animals in the zoo) will make the exotic animals much more meaningful than if the children had never visited the zoo.

Using symbols or representations of real objects is a second level of learning and is effective to the degree that the learner has been exposed to the real entity. At the zoo you looked at the animals, while your brain took in the entire environment as well. All these sensory data become part of the animal memory and are activated when it is remembered. When you look at the picture of an elephant, the neural network you activate allows you to recall where you were when you saw one, how it smelled, the trumpeting sound it made, and perhaps the feel of the water the elephant sprayed on you. Without the concrete experience, the representation or symbol may have little meaning, no matter how much someone explains it to you. This is certainly true in schools, where students often are exposed to representational information that has no concrete antecedent. Textbooks are crammed with pictures of science experiments, photographs of people in other communities, diagrams of digestive systems, and other such symbols or representations of real things. While they may be visually appealing, they do not bring to the students'

Without the concrete experience, the representation or symbol may have little meaning no matter how much someone explains it to you.

minds the rich sensory information contained in a concrete experience, and therefore they have less meaning.

Abstract Learning

A third level of learning uses only abstract information, primarily words and numbers. Let's say you are now older and your parents no longer take you to the zoo or buy you picture books about animals. Is there any way you can expand your neural network of animals? It is probable that you can now discuss animals you've never seen, whether real or imaginary (such as the three-headed dog, Fluffy, in the Harry Potter series). How are you able to do this? By reading about them. With a strong neural network formed both by concrete experience and representations of animals, it is possible to read about an animal and *see* it in your "mind's eye." Many abstract concepts have no visible concrete counterpart, such as "democracy" or "culture." An understanding of these terms will depend on the student's developmental age and on the teacher's ability to give sufficient examples that relate to the students' experiences and to involve students in experiences that make the abstract concepts understandable.

Involving Students in Real-Life Problem Solving

Many of our strongest neural networks are formed by actual experience. It is often possible to take advantage of this natural proclivity by involving students in solving authentic problems in their school or community. John Dewey (1937) contended that school should be less about preparation for life and more like life itself. While most school goals contain references to developing critical-thinking and problem-solving skills, they are not typically addressed in the classroom. Numerous studies indicate that indicate that "lecture-recitation" is still the primary mode of instruction in many classrooms (Goodlad, 1984; Hoetker & Ahlbrand, 1969; Sirotnik, 1983). Even when teachers give students the opportunity to solve problems, these "problems" are seldom more than hypothetical case studies with neat, convergent outcomes. With a little research and creative thinking, teachers can find actual problems in their own schools and communities for the students to solve. These real problems may not be easy to solve because of time constraints or insufficient information, but it is through struggling with these issues that students learn both content and critical thinking. Following are several examples of methods teachers have used in an attempt to increase authentic problem solving.

John Dewey contended that school should be less about preparation for life and more like life itself.

Lower Elementary School

A 3rd grade class was brainstorming what they needed to do to prepare for an upcoming field trip. When the issue of transportation was raised, one of the students suggested that their parents could drive and save the school the costs of busses. The teacher challenged the students to determine whether this would indeed be true. The students were divided into two groups, and each group set out to determine the costs involved in each mode of transportation. Students made calculations regarding the number of vehicles needed to transport the students, insurance costs for private cars versus school busses, and fuel costs per mile for each type of vehicle. Another problem-solving opportunity arose when one student questioned whether there would be enough parents available to drive on the day of the field trip. The problem was solved when the children determined that there were not enough parents who would be able to drive; but the real benefit to the students was not the solution but the data collection, analysis, and problem-solving skills they had gained.

Upper Elementary School

Students in a 5th grade class were challenged by their teacher to determine whether public opinion in their city matched that of the nation in a public poll regarding the selection of a presidential candidate. The students researched how polls are conducted, studied data collection, and learned how to form questions. After conducting a minipoll at their local shopping mall, they tabulated their results, compared them to the national results, and discussed the reasons for the differences. The local newspaper reported their efforts.

Middle School

A teacher in a California town read to his students a news story, which noted that human consumption accounted for a small percentage of the state's water usage, while landscaping and agriculture used much more. He challenged his students to find a way to conserve the limited water supply. After doing some research, the students discovered that some species of plants use much less water than others. They eventually drafted a water conservation bill requiring all new state buildings to be landscaped with drought-resistant plants. They convinced their local senator to sponsor the bill, which they calculated would save taxpayers both millions of dollars and gallons of water. They wrote letters to newspapers, prepared press kits, made all the arrangements for a press conference, and went to the state capitol to testify in support of their bill.

Secondary School

In a school-to-career program, teachers contact local businesses and ask them to identify problems they need to have solved. They then challenge groups of students in the program to find possible solutions. The students determine what information they need and set up interviews with the business owners to gain a better understanding of their problems. After analyzing their data, the students brainstorm solutions and select those they consider the most feasible. As a final step, they present their solution to the business owners. The teachers report that in the first year of the program most of the students' solutions have been implemented. In addition to the obvious benefits of engaging in authentic problem solving, teachers report that it also immeasurably enhances the students' motivation, sense of efficacy, and self-esteem.

All Levels

Creative teachers have reported numerous other examples of problem solving using community and school resources to increase the meaning of what they are teaching. Many of the problems facing our communities and our world can be used to involve students in critical thinking and problem solving. Examples are protecting natural habitats, issues surrounding the homeless, the spread of infectious diseases, how to keep teens from smoking, improving the quality of food offerings in the cafeteria, effects of global warming, and reducing freeway congestion. Problem solving can be an effective way to address classroom behavioral and academic issues at the same time. One teacher challenged her 6th grade students to find a way to improve their own math scores. A band director asked his students to find a way to purchase new band uniforms. In response to students' questions about when they would ever need what they were learning, an algebra teacher suggested they research which professions require a knowledge of algebra and how they use it.

An excellent source of authentic problems is a curriculum development and delivery system called problem-based learning (PBL). Numerous books and Internet sites outline the program and suggested curricula for all grade levels and subject areas (e.g.,

In addition to the obvious benefits of engaging in authentic problem solving, teachers report that it also immeasurably enhances students' motivation, sense of efficacy, and self-esteem.

Brandt, 1998; Center for Problem-Based Learning, 2001; Delisle, 1997; Torp & Sage, 1998).

Using Projects to Increase Meaning and Motivation

Watching students busily engaged in an activity is always a rewarding sight. When compared to sitting and listening to the teacher talk, student involvement in a project or experiment appears to be a much better way to learn. Indeed, projects and activities have rich potential as a means of engaging students and increasing understanding. However, caution is warranted when deciding when and how to use them. Too often we select activities that look like a lot of fun without considering what it is we want our students to gain from doing them. For example, in a study of early missions in California, a teacher instructed her students to construct missions out of sugar cubes. The students enjoyed this project and may have learned something about using sugar cubes as a building material; however, I wonder what working on this project taught the students about the effects of the missions on the Native Americans, the contributions of these settlements, or the role the missions played in California history..

Projects and activities should be a means to enhance learning, not an end in themselves. An activity should relate directly to a clearly defined objective or standard, not just superficially relate to it. Students need to be helped to understand the purpose of the project or activity. This can be done through an initial discussion or during the processing or debriefing at the close of the activity or completion of the project. Given these caveats, let's look at some examples of carefully planned and executed projects.

Lower Elementary School

Even younger children can become meaningfully involved in projects. A teacher in Oregon decided to tackle the issue of violence with her 2nd graders. After students had brainstormed examples of violence, they watched several children's television programs and tallied the acts of violence, which included threats, hitting, kicking, and bombs and other weapons, and reported their findings to their classmates. A reporter heard about their project and recommended that they contact a member of the County Board of Commissioners, which had as a priority the reduction of youth violence. He visited the classroom and brainstormed with the children how they could communicate their research results to others. As a result of this meeting, the children wrote a "Declaration of Independence from Violence," which included a pledge to boycott products advertised by shows that contained excessive violence. They contacted radio and other media, wrote letters to U.S. senators and representatives, and eventually were featured on ABC World News Tonight (Evans, 1996).

Upper Elementary School

While not necessarily based on solving problems, projects offer many of the same benefits in making the curriculum more meaningful to students. These activities often arise from student questions or interest about a topic they are studying. A 4th grade class had been studying the Native Americans who introduced the Pilgrims to corn. During their study of corn and its importance to the early colonists, the students determined that a corn muffin would be an excellent choice for state muffin. They researched the workings of government, wrote letters, and eventually lobbied the Massachusetts State House and testified before a legislative committee. The entire class was present to watch their bill signed into law by the governor of their state.

While not necessarily based on solving problems, projects offer many of the same benefits in making the curriculum more meaningful to students.

A teacher in Arizona developed a unique project to teach the culture of the native Hohokam people. His 5th grade students built a simulated archaeological site on the grounds of their school. After researching the Hohokam culture, they proceeded to build a multiroom, full-size housing site out of adobe bricks made on the school campus. In the following years, other students were involved in an archaeological dig of the site. Students learned proper methods of excavation and used written logs to enter all the data on each artifact they found. At the conclusion of the dig, the students put together a book giving information on each artifact and their conclusions on what the people were like who might have lived there. They also made more artifacts and reburied the ones they had already found, so the site could be used by the next class. The teacher reports that this project is unparalleled in teaching about the Native American culture in their community.

Middle School

A special education class studying the Great Depression found it difficult to obtain first-hand information about what it was like to live during that time. The teacher contacted senior citizens in a mobile home park and asked if they would be willing to be interviewed. Upon receiving a positive response, she had the students determine what they wanted to know, write and edit questions, then set a time convenient for the seniors to be interviewed. Later in the year, during a discussion about living on a fixed income, the students asked to interview the seniors a second time. The teacher reported that an unexpected side benefit of this project was a bonding between the seniors and the students. The students prepared and served a potluck dinner for their new friends, and the seniors began a volunteer program to assist the students in the classroom.

Secondary School

A team of students in an advanced English course decided to raise awareness and eliminate misconceptions about the homeless in their community, a suburb of Chicago. They surveyed 100 business owners and employees and found that 54 percent of the respondents thought there was a real homelessness problem, and 20 percent thought it affected their business. The team devised a brochure presenting the survey results, along with facts about homeless persons in their community and local resources to call. Other students in the program have tackled school issues such as crowded hallways and the attendance policy. Their teacher believes that they are getting a true sense of how to define and deal with real-world issues.

While problems and projects can be powerful learning experiences, what is learned does not necessarily transfer to new problems or settings. Students solving a problem in one context often fail to transfer what they've learned to a different context. One way to deal with this issue is to provide students with an additional, similar case and assist them in seeing the similarities. In this way students can learn to identify general principals or the "big ideas" that are transferable. Another method to increase the probability of transfer is to engage the students in a "what if" scenario: "What if this part of the problem were changed or the variables were different?" (National Research Council, 1999).

Simulations and Role Plays as Meaning Makers

It is unrealistic to expect that all curriculum topics can be addressed through authentic problem solving and projects. At times these activities are neither desirable nor feasible. In those situations, simulations become useful teaching strategies. Simulations are not real events, and they need to be carefully

One 2nd grade teacher helps her students understand what the various marks do by having them "walk the punctuation" as they read silently.

planned and processed for the full benefits to be realized. Students often need assistance in comparing and contrasting the simulation with the actual event so they can abstract the general principals from it. Experts in experiential learning tell us that the time spent in debriefing a simulation should be equal to the time spent in the activity itself. Some simulations are highly emotional, and while this can be an added benefit for retention, there is a potential danger when students aren't able to separate the simulation from reality and become upset or angry. In some cases, such as simulating the spread of HIV, parents should be made aware of the planned activity. Teachers also need to know when to stop an activity if students are becoming too emotional.

Lower Elementary School

Punctuation is often meaningless to young children. One 2nd grade teacher helps her students understand what the various marks do by having them "walk the punctuation" as they read silently. They pause when they reach a comma, stop for a period, shrug their shoulders for a question mark, and jump if the sentence ends in an exclamation mark. A 3rd grade teacher gives her students an opportunity to demonstrate how apostrophes are used in contractions by acting them out. Students stand in a line holding separate letter cards that form the two words to be contracted, such as "is" and "not." One student, acting as the apostrophe, moves to the letter "o" and asks it to leave as he is its replacement. The "o" moves out, the apostrophe moves into its place, the letters move together, and the contraction "isn't" has been formed. This same teacher makes learning punctuation fun by asking the students to generate sounds to represent different punctuation marks (à la Victor Borge) and sound out sentences and dialogue.

Upper Elementary School

Students in a 4th grade classroom in Alberta, Canada, decided to simulate an oil spill to determine which substances did the best job of removing the oil from the water and from the birds that may have been contaminated. They filled bowls with oil-covered water and dipped cotton balls (representing the birds) into the water. The students noted that the oil clung to the ball, leaving no part of it untouched. After testing several substances, they found that peat moss absorbed most of the oil when sprinkled on the surface of the water. This time the cotton ball "bird" came out of the water with only a few bits of peat moss and almost no oil. The teacher asked the students who they thought needed to know this information; they determined that the prime minister of Canada was the most likely person, and they set out to design a packet of materials to send to him. It included a videotape of students conducting and explaining their experiment, a formal write-up of the experiment, close-up still photographs of the "bird" before and after cleanup, and a cover letter explaining why they were sending this packet to him.

To help students understand the counterintuitive fact that sound travels faster through a solid than a gas, one 5th grade teacher has several students "become" molecules by first distributing themselves far apart, as in a gas, and then close together, as in a solid. One student represents a sound and touches the first molecule and says, "Beep." This molecule then touches the next, and so on, until the sound has traveled through all the molecules. The students quickly see how much faster the sound travels through the closely spaced molecules representing a solid.

Our brains have difficulty comprehending very large numbers because we have nothing in our experience to "hook" them to.

Middle School

Students in a certain middle school pre-algebra class spend little time at their desks solving equations with pencil and paper.

Instead, they engage in an exercise in "human graphing," finding their places as coordinates on X and Y axes marked on the floor with masking tape. Students observing the activity sketch and describe the shape they see. On another day, they walk a large number line painted on the floor to simulate the addition and subtraction of integers. In a social studies classroom, students are absorbed drawing pictures of workers in a simulation of an assembly line. In the debriefing following the simulation, the students eagerly discuss the pros and cons of assembly line work (Teachers' Curriculum Institute, 1999). In still another classroom, middle school students are using their well-known energy simulating the process of photosynthesis, while it is being videotaped to show parents at an open house.

Our brains have difficulty comprehending large numbers because we have nothing in our experience to "hook" them to. Helping students comprehend the distribution of the Earth's population and resources often is an exercise in memorizing meaningless statistics. But in one 8th grade classroom, students are involved in a simulation to bring these data to life. The teacher divides the classroom into six major political/geographic regions and assigns students to "populate" each region in the same proportion as in the world today. The teacher then distributes matchbooks to represent energy consumption, peanuts for protein, and Hershey's Kisses for wealth. Students can easily identify with the "haves" and "have nots" of the world when they see the people in the North America region with a highly disproportionate amount of wealth, energy, and food. (A copy of the complete simulation, Food for Thought, is available from Zero Population Growth, 1400 16th St. NW, Washington, DC 29936.)

Secondary School

An English Literature teacher who was beginning a study of *Robin Hood* wanted her students to understand the historical context of the story, so she designed a simulation to accomplish this goal. She divided the class into two camps representing the Saxons and the Normans. She assigned four students the role of "historians" to objectively record the events. The "Saxons" were each given a small package of candy; the "Normans" received no candy. The teacher informed them that she was going to ask questions alternately of the two groups to determine a winner. If the "Saxons" answered the questions correctly they could keep the candy, and if the "Normans" were correct, they could take candy from the "Saxons." The questions, however, were rigged so that only the Normans were successful.

At the end of the simulation (when the "Normans" had all the candy), the teacher asked the "historians" to read their observations. They reported that the "Saxons" had tried to hide their candy, ruined the candy before giving it to the enemy, and angrily threw their candy at the "Normans." The "Normans" had gloated, taunted, and tried to take two packages of candy at a time. After having all students write their reflections in their journals, the teacher debriefed the activity with them. Students reported that they now understood why the Saxon thanes had burned their homes rather than let the Normans take them, and how conflicts often are unfair, with one side having more resources than the other. The reading of *Robin Hood*, the teacher reports, was much more meaningful to these students than it had been to students in previous classes.

To make the composition of an element more meaningful, a science teacher took his class out to the football field and divided them into three groups, each representing either protons, neutrons, or electrons. "Neutrons" stood making a big "O" with their hands over their heads, representing a neutral charge. The students representing protons became positive by making crosses with their arms, and those representing electrons took an Egyptian stance, with arms pointed front and back to represent a negative charge. The teacher called out the name of an element, and the students ran to the appropriate positions to simulate its composition.

All Levels

Setting up a business in the classroom in which students produce a product is a simulation that provides experience in planning, marketing, accounting, production scheduling, and banking. Some school districts, with help from local attorneys and judges, have implemented peer courts, where students learn about the judicial system in an authentic setting. Simulating a grocery store in the classroom (where shelves are stocked with empty food containers) gives elementary students experience in planning meals, reading labels, staying within a budget, and making change. While simulations require additional planning and work on the part of the teacher, they are an excellent way to increase meaning while being highly motivational and stimulating transfer of knowledge.

Synapse Strengtheners

1. Select a unit that you normally teach in a traditional manner and create a simulation to address its objectives. At the end of the unit, ask students for written feedback of their reactions and how presentation of the unit compared to the more traditional method.

2. If you are reading this book as a member of a study group, ask each member to interview teachers at his/her grade level for simulations they have used successfully. Compile these into a booklet and distribute them to the teachers in the school.

3. Prepare a response to a parent who wants to know why you are "playing games" in the classroom, rather than teaching in the more traditional method by which she was taught.

Using the Visual and Auditory Senses to Enhance Learning

9

T ake a moment and think about a particularly memorable event in your life. Perhaps you are recalling a special vacation spent at the beach or backpacking in the Sierras, or maybe you're thinking about your wedding day or the day your first child entered kindergarten. Whatever event comes to mind, you remember it not in words but in images and sounds. When you describe the event to someone else, you use words of course, but what you are describing is what you are seeing and hearing inside your head.

As we discussed in Chapter 5, Daniel Siegel explains that when you mentally "see" an image or "hear" a sound, you are reactivating or reconstructing the neural pathways that were formed when you first experienced the stimulus. In fact, it is nearly impossible not to recall the sights and sounds. If I say, "Picture an elephant or think about the 'ABC Song,'" you see an elephant or hear the song. If I say, "Do *not* picture an elephant or do *not* hear the 'ABC Song,' you still see the elephant or hear the song. These sensory abilities are powerful components of brain functioning, and we can use them in the classroom to enhance our students' understanding and retention of information.

A Picture Is Worth at Least 10,000 Words

Humans are intensely visual animals. The eyes contain nearly 70 percent of the body's sensory receptors and send millions of signals every second along the optic nerves to the visual processing centers of the brain. It is not surprising that the visual components of a memory are so robust. Although each of us has the ability to process kinesthetic and auditory information, we take in more information visually than through any of the other senses.

"I Never Forget a Face"

Several studies validate how well the mind processes and remembers visual information. One of the most remarkable was a study conducted in 1973 by Lionel Standing at Bishop's University in Canada. He presented volunteers with 10,000 photographic slides depicting a variety of subject matter. The volunteers viewed each picture for five seconds each over a period of five days. At the end of the fifth day, they were tested with a random sample of 160 out of the full set of 10,000. Researchers paired the pictures they had seen with ones they had not seen; and for each pair, the volunteers had to choose the picture they had seen before. Remarkably, the subjects selected the correct picture about 73 percent of the time (Squire & Kandel, 2000; Standing, 1973).

In a similar study, the investigators showed subjects photographs of classmates two months after graduation. Not surprisingly, the subjects were able to recognize 90 percent of those who had been in their class. The amazing fact is that the recognition rate was still close to 90 percent when they were tested 15 years later. The capacity for long-term memory of pictures seems almost unlimited (Bahrick, Bahrick, & Wittlinger,1976).

The fact that images are memorable is supported not only by the research but by our own observations. When we are having

The eyes contain nearly 70 percent of the body's sensory receptors and send millions of signals every second along the optic nerves to the visual processing centers of the brain.

difficulty recalling something, we often explain our failure as an inability to "picture" it. You've probably had the experience of taking a test and trying to recall the information that was represented by a chart or drawing. You could "see" the chart and remember where on the page it is located, and with a little luck you might even be able to recall the information it contains. The importance of visualizing is also evident in many common metaphors, such as "I see what you mean" or "He can't see the forest for the trees."

Thinking in Pictures

Not only are visuals powerful retention aids, but they also serve to increase understanding. Imagine trying to comprehend the structure of an atom without a drawing or to understand the operation of an internal combustion engine without an accompanying diagram. The ability to transform thoughts into images is often viewed as a test of true understanding. But some people appear to process information the other way around, literally seeming to comprehend information by visualizing it. One such person was Albert Einstein, who appeared to process information primarily in images, rather than in written words or spoken language. He wrote that all his ideas came to him in more or less clear images, and that he had great difficulty putting his ideas into words (Shaw, 2000). Another such person is Temple Grandin, a Professor of Animal Science at Colorado State University and a leading expert in the design of livestock-handling facilities. Temple is autistic. In her autobiography, *Thinking in Pictures*, she explains that her only avenue to understanding abstract concepts is through picturing them (Grandin, 1995).

In his book *Keeping Mozart in Mind*, physicist Gordon Shaw discusses how critical spatial-temporal reasoning is for comprehending math and science concepts (Shaw, 2000). One of the defining characteristics of this type of reasoning is the ability to

The capacity for long-term memory of pictures seems almost unlimited.

Using a keyword imagery mnemonic process, in which subjects linked the sound of the word to an image of a concrete noun in English, researchers increased college students' retention of Spanish vocabulary words from 28 percent to 88 percent.

transform abstract concepts into visual images. Perhaps this is why students in the 5th grade have such difficulty with multiplying and dividing fractions. It is very difficult for most students to create a mental picture of 1/4 x 1/3. (It can be done if you understand that 1/4 x 1/3 really means 1/4 *of* 1/3 of a whole.) Shaw and his colleagues have collected impressive data showing that piano keyboard training, taught in conjunction with a computer program that uses images to depict math and science concepts, dramatically increases elementary students' math understanding and test scores. A later section of this chapter addresses the music aspect of this research.

Many studies have shown the facilitating effect of imagery, especially pictures, on learning and memory. One study examined 6th graders' understanding and recall of vocabulary words using two different strategies. One group memorized dictionary definitions of the words, while a second group drew their own pictures of them. The second group's retention of the words was much higher (Bull & Wittrock, 1973). Using a keyword imagery mnemonic process, in which subjects linked the sound of the word to an image of a concrete noun in English, researchers increased college students' retention of Spanish vocabulary words from 28 percent to 88 percent (Atkinson & Raugh, 1975; Raugh & Atkinson, 1975).

Classroom Strategies Using Visual Processing

Elementary School. Using visuals or imagery with young children sometimes presents problems because of the students' limited drawing skills. "Imposed visuals," in which the student uses an image provided by the teacher, will often be necessary for children in kindergarten and 1st grade. For older students, however, "induced visuals," in which students generate their own images, are generally more effective.

In their 1st grade team, a group of teachers designed a "gallon person," with the body representing a gallon, the arms and legs being one quart each, the wrists and ankles making up eight pints (two each), and four digits on each hand and foot representing cups. A 2nd grade teacher, looking for a way to help her students understand and remember that every word has a vowel in it, created a bulletin board that contained six houses with doors that his students could open. Inside each door "lived" one of the five vowels or "Y."

Teachers can help students understand the correct placement of quotation marks in written dialogue by drawing a happy face on the board and placing the quotation marks at the corners of the mouth. (See Figure 9.1.)

Middle School. A science teacher instructs students to take notes in a "split page" formation. On the left-hand side of the page, the students take notes on what they are reading, and on the right they draw a picture to represent what they have written.

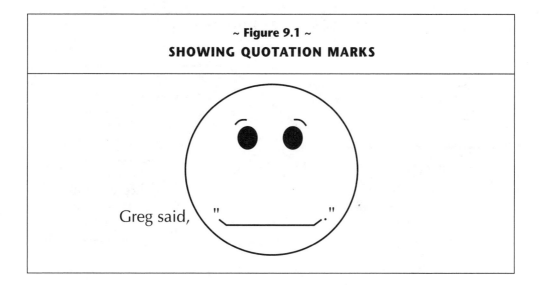

~ Figure 9.1 ~
SHOWING QUOTATION MARKS

Students in a math class were asked to determine which of the following decimals had the greatest value—.08, .8, .080, or .008000—and to explain their answer. Most of the students picked the correct answer (.8), but their explanations (".8 is the greatest because it has no zeros before or after it") demonstrated that they lacked an understanding of the concept. The teacher then had the students create a drawing that illustrated these values and had them share their drawings in groups. This resulted in an animated discussion as the students discovered how many different ways this concept could be correctly illustrated.

A middle school English teacher helps her students understand the framework for a short story by graphically representing the plot on a diagram. (See Figure 9.2.)

Secondary School. A freshman English teacher decided to involve her students more actively in their weekly vocabulary lessons by letting them choose partners to help them teach their

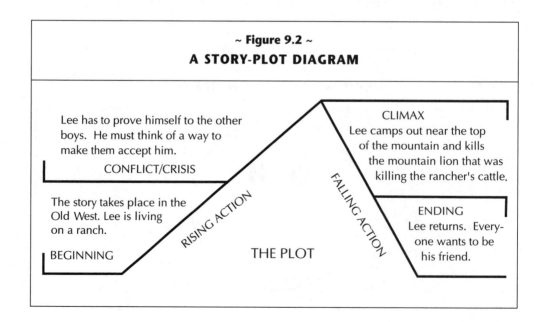

~ Figure 9.2 ~
A STORY-PLOT DIAGRAM

Lee has to prove himself to the other boys. He must think of a way to make them accept him.

CONFLICT/CRISIS

The story takes place in the Old West. Lee is living on a ranch.

BEGINNING

RISING ACTION

THE PLOT

CLIMAX
Lee camps out near the top of the mountain and kills the mountain lion that was killing the rancher's cattle.

FALLING ACTION

ENDING
Lee returns. Everyone wants to be his friend.

classmates an assigned word. She challenged the teams to present their word in such a way that everyone in the class would remember the word, not just for the test, but "for the rest of their lives." She was surprised to discover that their two- to three-minute presentations were extremely creative and that the students thoroughly enjoyed this novel way of studying vocabulary. Many of her students chose to use posters or the chalkboard to visually represent their words. Two girls displayed a lovely, drooping rose, explaining that it was a sad rose and should be recalled when the word *morose* is read. Another pair created a giant report card with an *F* in every subject and called on their teacher to be the 9th grade recipient of the card. She was instructed to act *disconsolate*, which was the word the students had been assigned.

The structure of these frameworks resembles the structure used by the brain to organize information.

The History Alive! curriculum suggests having students expand their note-taking and understanding by keeping an interactive notebook. (See Figure 9.3.) Periodically during a lecture or during their reading, the teacher asks students to interact with their notes using one of several suggested alternatives. Some options are to create a map or web of the content, draw a cartoon, or sketch a particular scene. Teachers using this technique report that it results in increased retention and understanding of the content being studied (Teachers' Curriculum Institute, 1999).

All Levels. Many teachers use graphics to help students organize their thinking. Called *mind* or *thinking* maps, webs, clusters, network trees, fishbone maps, or graphic organizers, they have proved to be particularly effective at increasing students' understanding and retention of information. Perhaps this is because these visual devices make it possible to see connections between aspects of the information that are not obvious in a linear form, such as an outline or a narrative. The structure of these frameworks resembles the structure used by the brain to organize information.

Brain
Matters: Translating Research into Classroom Practice

Remember that the various aspects of a memory, or of a learned fact, are not stored in a single, specific location in the brain, but are stored in networks of networks. Images are stored in the visual cortex, sounds in the auditory cortex, and so forth. This may be why visually mapping information has proved productive for enhancing students' storage and retention of information: It mirrors the structure used by the brain.

Teachers can select from many visual structures, depending on the desired outcome. They can use graphics, called advanced

~ Figure 9.3 ~

AN INTERACTIVE NOTEBOOK

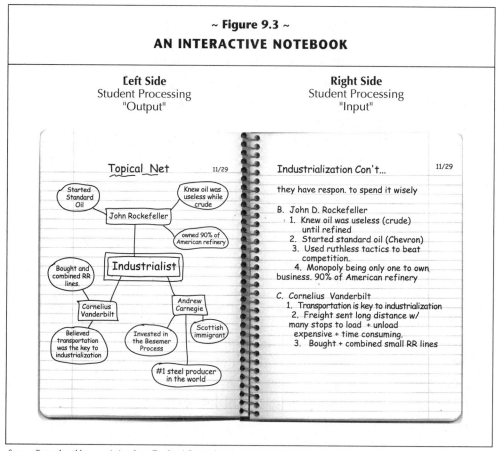

Left Side
Student Processing
"Output"

Right Side
Student Processing
"Input"

Source: Reproduced by permission from Teachers' Curriculum Institute. (1999). *History alive! Engaging all learners in the diverse classroom* (2nd ed.). Mountain View, CA: Author p. 127.

organizers, to help students organize information in a predetermined format. Figure 9.4 shows an example that a teacher has
structured to help students focus on essential aspects of a chapter
in an environmental science text.

Another visual organizer is the familiar web or bubble map.
These organizers have a number of uses. They can be used before
writing to help students brainstorm aspects of a topic they might
include in their composition. Or they may serve as a way to dis-
play and organize what students know about a particular topic
before beginning a unit of study. Another application is as a
framework for organizing main ideas and subtopics as students
read information in a text. Figure 9.5 is an example of a "double-
bubble" map drawn to help students organize information about
Julius Caesar's private and public lives. *A Field Guide to Using
Visual Tools* (Hyerle, 2000) is an excellent source of information
regarding the many forms of graphics and their use in
educational settings.

~ Figure 9.4 ~
AN ADVANCED ORGANIZER

Biome	Climate	Main Plants	Main Animals	Human Activities	Environmental Problems
Tropical rainforest					
Desert					
Temperate grasslands					

Brain
Matters: Translating Research into Classroom Practice

Music (Rhyme and Rhythm) Hath Many Charms

We tend to think of music only in cultural or artistic terms, but scientists have found that music is a highly complex neural activity. Sound waves enter our ears and are converted into nerve impulses by the Organ of Corti in the cochlea. From there, the impulses are transmitted to specialized regions in our left and right temporal lobes for processing. Suppose that the sounds entering our ears are the notes making up a symphony. For us to

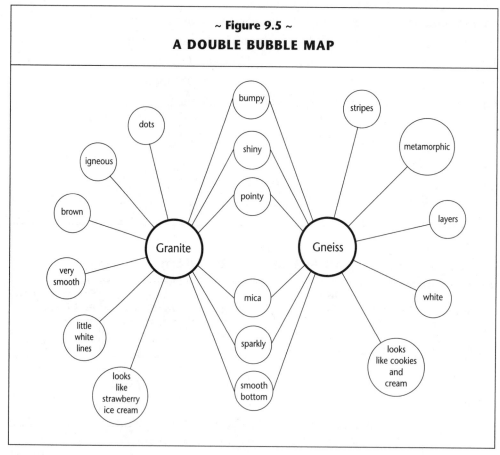

~ Figure 9.5 ~
A DOUBLE BUBBLE MAP

Source: Hyerle, D. (2000). *A field guide to using visual tools.* Alexandria, VA: Association for Supervision and Curriculum Development, p. 27.

make sense of the music, the signals must travel from the temporal lobes to working memory in the frontal lobes. Sounds unfold over time, and our brains must be able to hold on to a sequence of sounds for several seconds or minutes in order to compare them with new sounds arriving in the brain. This is what working memory does so well. It allows us to hold the musical information over a period of time to decode it. The frontal lobes are where the sounds are recognized as patterns of notes and musical phrases that make up sonatas and symphonies.

Contrary to the popular misconception that music is the property of the right hemisphere, new imaging techniques have shown that music is distributed across specialized regions in both hemispheres. In fact, many musical experiences can activate the cognitive, visual, auditory, affective, and motor systems, depending on whether you are reading music, playing an instrument, composing a song, beating out a rhythm, or just listening to a melody.

The mental mechanisms that process music are deeply entwined with the brain's other basic functions, including emotion, memory, and even language. Research shows that the human brain is predisposed to detect patterns in both music and language. It is interesting that we appear to favor certain types of musical patterns over others. Canadian researcher Sandra Trehub has found that infants prefer consonant to dissonant passages. Four-month-old infants demonstrate a preference for hearing Mozart sonatas as originally written, compared to "unnatural" versions (Krumhansl & Jusczyk, 1996).

The mental mechanisms that process music are deeply entwined with the brain's other basic functions, including emotion, memory, and even language.

Music and Emotion

Music's emotional impact is well documented. Robert Zatorre, a neuroscientist at McGill University in Montreal, used PET scans to examine cerebral blood flow changes related to affective responses to music. He found that the parts of the brain involved in processing emotion "light up" with activity when a subject hears music (Blood, Aztorre, Bermudez, & Evans, 1999). It is not surprising that music can incite a broad range of emotions, including passion, serenity, or fear. Most of us can recall instances when music induced changes in our own emotional level, perhaps when we listened to Handel's "Hallelujah Chorus" or the background music in a movie thriller. The reason for the emotional arousal appears to be that music affects levels of several brain chemicals, including epinephrine, endorphins, and cortisol, the hormone involved in the "fight-or-flight" response. In Chapter 6 we saw that one of the links between emotion and memory involves these same neurotransmitters and hormones. Perhaps this is why a mere snippet of a song from our past can trigger highly vivid memories.

There is little doubt that when information is embedded in music or rhyme, its recall is enhanced.

You Must Remember This . . .

If you are of a certain age, the preceding phrase will result in the automatic response, "a kiss is still a kiss." No matter what your age, if you grew up speaking English environment, you can most likely complete the following: "In fourteen hundred and ninety-two . . ."; "Thirty days hath September . . ."; "Plop, plop, fizz, fizz . . ."; "M-I-C, K-E-Y . . ."; or "Humpty Dumpty sat on a wall . . . ." There is little doubt that when information is embedded in music or rhyme, its recall is enhanced. People can typically remember lyrics of tunes and rhymes, but are much less successful in recalling prose passages.

Although many scientists believe that language and music are closely linked and share some of the same neural circuits, music (or rhyme set to music) clearly has the advantage when it comes to recall. We can use this natural proclivity of the brain in designing educational activities that will enhance the retention of certain kinds of information.

Music, Mozart, and Math

By now almost everyone has heard of the "Mozart Effect." Various news media and popular magazines have touted it as a way to enhance relaxation, increase concentration, boost intelligence in babies, and make the listener a whiz in math. But the original study that spawned those stories made no such claims. In 1993, physicist Gordon Shaw and his colleagues at the University of California-Irvine, reported in the journal *Nature* that college students who listened to the Mozart "Sonata for Two Pianos in D Major" did better on reasoning tasks than after listening to a relaxation tape or silence (Shaw, 2000). But the results lasted only 10 minutes. The report, however, captured the imagination of people around the world as an effortless way to boost intelligence; and it resulted in countless articles, books, and recordings' making claims that often had not been substantiated.

Although people have widely misinterpreted the Mozart Effect, researchers have found that music does have certain beneficial effects on learning. Shaw believes that music uses many of the same higher brain functions as math and science and that training in music can enhance these functions. He and Frances Rauscher, at the University of Wisconsin, have conducted a number of additional studies that examine the link between music training and spatial-temporal reasoning (Shaw, 2000). Spatial-temporal reasoning is the ability to visualize a problem and a solution; it generally results in increased conceptual understanding of the problem. Temple Grandin, mentioned earlier in this chapter, is gifted in this type of reasoning.

Shaw's studies have produced amazing results. Shaw and his colleagues have developed an interactive math software program called Spatial-Temporal Animation Reasoning (STAR), which allows children to solve geometric and math puzzles that increase their ability to manipulate shapes in their minds. Combining instruction on piano keyboards with the STAR training resulted in inner-city 2nd graders' scoring 27 percent higher in proportional math and fractions than other children who took English language instruction on the computer and worked only with STAR software. Half the 2nd graders scored as well as 5th graders in a more affluent, neighboring district; and they scored twice as high as the children without either training (Shaw, 2000). Though the computer game played an important role in enhancing spatial-temporal reasoning, the music appears to be the determining factor, because the lower-scoring students also played the computer game.

Using Music, Rhyme, and Rhythm in the Classroom

Teachers can find many avenues for using music to enhance both the classroom environment and student learning. Certain types of music affect brain wave patterns, resulting in a slowing down or speeding up of brain activity. Some teachers report that playing music such as Handel's *Water Music Suite* or Vivaldi's *Four Seasons* soothes and calms their students, whereas marches have an opposite, energizing effect. These same selections also could be used to increase students' ability to analyze musical sounds and patterns and to develop an understanding of how composers communicate through their music. In the same vein, elementary students enjoy learning to identify the characters portrayed by different instruments in Tchaikovsky's *Peter and the Wolf.*

Music can be a powerful approach for integrating various curricular areas. The patterns and symbols in music are underlying concepts that help to make math more understandable. For example, one natural link is to teach students about fractions as they learn the values of whole, half, and quarter notes. We can enhance the study of history by looking at the effects of patriotic songs on peoples' emotions and actions. Students can gain increased understanding of communication from learning how

Students can gain increased understanding of communication from learning how people have used drum rhythms and songs of traveling minstrels to disseminate information or elements of a culture from one place to another.

people have used drum rhythms and songs of traveling minstrels to disseminate information or elements of a culture from one place to another. In a film and drama class, students can experience and document how different types of music affect their mood as they watch a horror film. An environmental science teacher asks his students to map the food chain described in Pete Seeger's folk song, "The People Are Scratchin'." As part of the final assessment for a unit, this same teacher gives his students the option of demonstrating their understanding of an ecological concept they have been studying by producing a music video.

Rhyme and rhythm provide great mechanisms for storing information that would otherwise be difficult to retain. As mentioned earlier, information embedded in music or rhyme is much easier to recall than the same information in prose. Think about very young children who are able to repeat dozens of nursery rhymes and songs they've learned on Sesame Street. In Chapter 6, we learned that 5-year-old children can work consciously with approximately two bits of information at a time, which would seem to put severe limits on the capacity of their memories. Nearly all children in kindergarten, however, can sing the "ABC Song," which strings together 26 bits of data that have no intrinsic relationship to each other. (It is noteworthy that the tune to this song, "Twinkle, Twinkle, Little Star," was composed by Mozart.)

Rhyme and rhythm are great methods for storing information that would otherwise be difficult to retain.

Piggyback Songs

The "ABC Song" is an example of what is sometimes called a *piggyback* song—a song in which new words or concepts are set to a familiar melody. Young children often lack the ability to create their own piggyback songs, but they quickly learn to sing songs taught to them by their parents or teachers. One 1st grade teacher helps her students remember how to end a sentence by teaching them the "Period Song," to the tune of "Row, Row, Row Your Boat":

Stop, stop, stop the words
With a little dot.
Use a period at the end,
So they'll know to stop.

Another example of a piggyback song is "The Continent Song," sung to the tune of *"Frere Jacques."* This song also uses motion of body parts to show the general locations of the continents.

North America (hold up left hand),
Europe (point to nose),
Asia (hold up right hand),
Africa, Africa (make a circle around the waist
    with both hands),
South America (point to left knee),
Australia (point to right knee)
Antarctica, Antarctica (stomp feet).

Adding movement to the music or rhyme provides an extra sensory input to the brain and probably enhances the learning.

In that example, adding movement to the music or rhyme provides an extra sensory input to the brain and probably enhances the learning. Rhymes to teach spelling or punctuation rules, names of planets, parts of the human body, and so forth, can all be set to jump-rope jingles or other movements.

Remembering how to spell a word also is easier if you sing it to a familiar tune. Five-letter words can be sung to the tune of "You Are My Sunshine"; six-letter words fit the tune of "Happy Birthday to You," and seven-letter words can be sung to the tune of "Twinkle, Twinkle, Little Star." Piggyback songs are also a preferred learning strategy in many foreign language and bilingual classes. I can still remember learning the numerals and months of the year in Spanish by singing *"Uno de enero, dos de febrero, tres de marzo, quatro de abril"* to the tune of "San Fermin."

Rhythm, Rhyme, and Rap

Learning content by embedding it in music or rhyme is generally more effective if students are involved in creating the product, rather than using one composed by someone else. In a Driver's Education class in Illinois, I watched students as they demonstrated their knowledge of the operating systems of the automobile through songs set to the tunes of their favorite songs or to rap. One group of boys explained the braking system of a car to the tune of "YMCA," with all the appropriate motions included, and a group of girls entertained the class with a rap of the cooling system. In an environmental science class, students wrote riddles about various chemical elements such as "I'm the lightest of gases, I'm found in all stars. Touch me with a match, and I'll blow them apart! What am I?" They then used these verses to quiz other students.

Upper elementary and middle school teachers often find that many students have difficulty memorizing the multiplication tables. The twos, fives, and tens are usually the easiest, perhaps because many teachers have taught students to count in rhythm by these numbers. The rhythmic counting quickly becomes automatic. All the multiplication tables would likely be learned more quickly if we taught students to count by all numbers, not just by twos, fives, and tens. But even with our best efforts, some students still have difficulty. One middle-school teacher charged with helping a group of 8th graders pass a required test on the multiplication tables faced this problem. Knowing that these students probably wouldn't be too excited about singing to the tune of "Three Blind Mice," she suggested they put the multiplication tables in a rap. They did so, and it wasn't long before they had mastered all the tables and made a tape of their rap called "Tough Times," which they offered to their peers.

Learning content by embedding it in music or rhyme is generally more beneficial when students are involved in creating the product, rather than using one composed by someone else.

An expectation of many 1st grade students is that they will learn to read on the first day of school. One creative teacher fulfills this expectation using a simple song that she has duplicated in a little booklet for each child. She has the children sing the song repeatedly throughout the day, color the pictures in their book, and practice singing and reading the song to each other. At the end of the day, each child reads the words of the song to her and receives a certificate stating that the child has learned to read on the first day of 1st grade.

Commercial Songs

Many songs, jingles, and raps are commercially available and can be used to teach a variety of concepts to students. Schools can purchase tapes and CDs to teach nouns and verbs, countries of the world, the order of the planets from the sun, the freedoms listed in the Constitution, and addition and subtraction facts. Although these can be beneficial teaching aids, there is probably more value in having students create or compose their own if they are able.

Synapse Strengtheners

1. Select a concept that your students normally have difficulty under-standing and design a graphic organizer for it. Give the students the major topics and subtopics that are going to be addressed and have them put them into the organizer. At the end of the unit, ask students whether it helped them organize their thoughts and better comprehend the concept.

2. If your study group started a booklet containing simulations, add to it by interviewing teachers and gathering examples of visuals, songs, rhymes, etc., that they have used successfully with their students.

3. Prepare a response to a colleague or a parent who has heard that listening to Mozart makes you smarter.

10 | A Toolkit of Brain-Compatible Strategies

The discussion of "rehearsal" in Chapter 6 noted that students need to practice some skills over and over to become proficient. There are no shortcuts to learning to read or to playing the flute; both require a great deal of rote rehearsal with guidance from a skilled teacher. These skills fall into the category of procedural memory—learning and remembering *how* to do something. For semantic memory—the nature and rules of language and mathematics, and our general knowledge about our world—rote rehearsal is generally much less effective. To store semantic information, a different type of rehearsal, called *elaborative rehearsal*, is needed.

This chapter describes strategies that elaborate on information to increase its meaning, as well as the probability of its retention. For the most part, these strategies are not new or esoteric; some—like mnemonics—have been used for thousands of years. But with an increased awareness of how the brain processes information, we are beginning to understand why these strategies work, and we can select those that fit the needs of students in particular learning situations.

Enhancing Understanding Through Writing Activities

There is a saying that "writing is nature's way of letting us see how sloppy our thinking is." Anyone who has written an article or a book knows just how true this is. Writing and thinking are strongly linked: Writing can serve as a tool for refining thinking. At the same time, complex, cognitive activity produces more articulate and expressive writing. Writing activities fit in the category of elaborative rehearsal because they challenge students to clarify, organize, and express what they are learning.

Writing to Learn Mathematics

At every grade level, students' understanding of mathematical concepts can be enhanced by writing about what they are studying. We can teach children in the primary grades to write simple sentences explaining equations. Figure 10.1 shows one 1st grader's understanding of addition in a problem he had generated.

The purpose of instruction in mathematics is to give students the skills they will need to solve real-life problems involving numbers. Texts typically include word problems to provide practice in problem solving. Too often however, these problems are abstract and meaningless. When students write their own word problems for others in the class to solve, the problems have more meaning and can be a lot of fun. Consider this problem written by a 4th grade student: "My teacher talks 50 miles an hour. In the first 45 minutes of class, how many miles has she talked?" Another student wrote, "I started out with 37 ants. I put 15 of them in my sister's bed and 16 in my mother's cookie dough. How many ants did I have left?"

There is a saying that "writing is nature's way of letting us see how sloppy our thinking is."

At every grade level, students' understanding of mathematical concepts can be enhanced by writing about what they are studying.

Brain
Matters: Translating Research into Classroom Practice

Middle and secondary students also can benefit from generating their own mathematical problems. A geometry teacher asked her students to create original theorems to help them understand the underlying structure of the problems in the text. Another secondary teacher has his students brainstorm money problems they face in their own lives, formulate them into a problem-solving format, and present them to the class. Their problems have centered on interest on credit card debt, expenses involved in purchasing and maintaining a car, and whether a part-time job is really profitable.

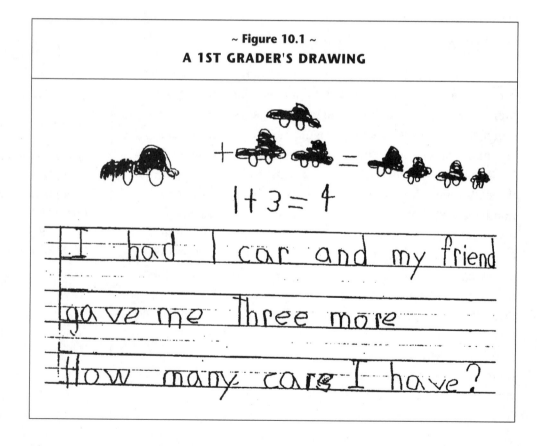

~ Figure 10.1 ~
A 1ST GRADER'S DRAWING

$$1 + 3 = 4$$

I had 1 car and my friend
gave me three more
How many cars I have?

Writing about what they are learning in math helps students make sense of the information by putting the ideas and methods they are using in their own words. Periodically, teachers can ask students to complete sentences such as "I'm really confused about . . . " and "Factoring is easy if . . . " and "I think calculators . . . ." Another strategy is to ask students to write a note to an absent classmate describing what they learned in class that day (Countryman, 1992).

Writing Strategies for History and Social Studies

Writing assignments in social studies or history at any grade level typically require students to research a country, an event, or a person and to write a paper. These assignments are often meaningless and result in some creative plagiarism, but little learning. Writing can be a motivating learning experience, however, if the student has something memorable to write about. Much of the success in writing depends on what has occurred before the student starts writing. When students see powerful slides or films, discuss a controversial issue, or act out a moment in history, they are gaining not only information but also motivation for writing.

In the History Alive! curriculum mentioned in Chapter 9, students work on many kinds of writing activities, such as dialogues, poetry, stories, newspaper eulogies, speeches, and letters. For example, suppose that the assignment is to write a dialogue between Martin Luther King Jr. and Malcolm X. The students first read, view, and discuss primary source material on the Civil Rights Movement. Then, working with a partner, they assume the role of either person and engage in a role-play designed to give them ideas for the dialogue. By the time the students are ready to write, they are much more likely to really understand the ideas of these two men and are much better prepared and motivated to write the dialogue (Teachers' Curriculum Institute, 1999).

Writing can be a motivating learning experience if the student has something memorable to write about.

During a study of World War I, students in History Alive! classrooms pretend to be soldiers in trenches writing letters to families at home. To get a feel for this event, the students write while sitting on the floor between rows of upside-down chairs to simulate trenches. A slide of a WWI battle projected on the wall in front of them adds to the atmosphere.

Other writing activities might include composing a memorandum to a historical leader that recommends a course of action or a new policy, writing a newspaper editorial about a historical event, or writing a eulogy extolling the virtues of a prominent historical figure. Although the History Alive! curriculum is designed for middle and secondary school use, students at all levels benefit from these types of writing experiences. Elementary students can assume the role of a person living in a particular time period or another part of the country and make entries in a diary that the person might have kept. Students can create a newsletter reporting "current" events that occurred during a period of history they are studying; teams of three or four students are responsible for different sections of the newsletter.

In a kindergarten class, students draw small pictures representing various activities that have taken place in their class that week, and they dictate a sentence to the teacher describing each one. The final product is a newsletter to parents of their classroom's "current events." Before taking them home at the end of the week, the students role-play "reading" the newsletter to their parents. This type of dictated writing is especially important for young children, as it allows them to see that what they say can be written.

Dictated writing is especially important for young children, as it allows them to see that what they say can be written.

Writing to Increase Understanding in Science

Although an understanding of scientific concepts is critical, the larger goal of science instruction is to help students learn to think and act like a scientist. Writing plays an important role in the life of scientists, because they must describe their hypotheses and experimental designs in a precise manner, carefully document each step of their studies, and accurately communicate their findings and conclusions to readers. An environmental science teacher teaches the importance of careful observation and accurate description by asking students to observe and write detailed descriptions of simple objects such as leaves. Other students try to identify the objects from their descriptions. In a similar activity, designed to stress the need for accurate written directions, this teacher directs the students to make three folds in a 3 x 5 card to create a certain shape and write directions for another student to follow that will result in the same shape.

In another school, an earth science teacher asks her students to assume the role of a space traveler on a tour of the solar system and to accurately describe what they observe for scientists on Earth. A biology teacher combines writing and drawing with an activity called Quick Write/Quick Draw. The example shown in Figure 10.2 is a student's description and drawing that summarize the process of photosynthesis.

At every grade level, students can find many ways to help clarify their thinking through writing. An important part of being a scientist is asking questions. Students can find answers to their questions from a variety of sources, but one of the most exciting is by direct communication with scientists. The Internet provides access to many scientists. For example, Eric Chudler, a research associate professor at the University of Washington in Seattle, routinely answers students' questions about the brain on a Web site called *Neuroscience for Kids* (http://faculty.washington.edu/ chudler/neurok.html). Writing to an actual scientist requires careful thought about what questions to ask and how to phrase them. This experience creates a great deal of excitement, as students eagerly check their e-mail for a response. They can also use the Internet to communicate with students in other parts of the

Brain
Matters: Translating Research into Classroom Practice

world to obtain firsthand information about climate, living conditions, food sources, flora and fauna, and so forth. In addition to collecting data, students can formulate hypotheses about why differences exist among regions, and work with their counterparts to correlate their data.

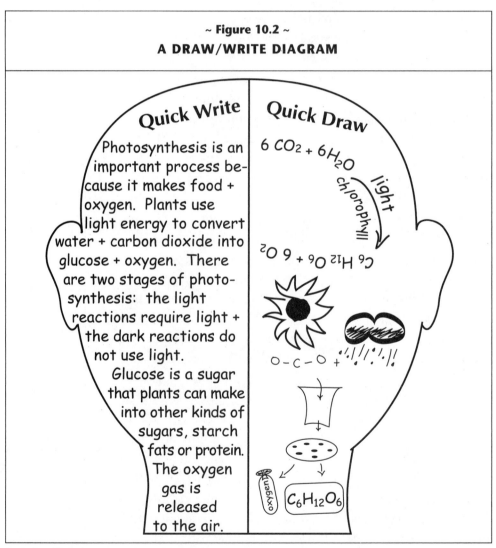

~ Figure 10.2 ~
A DRAW/WRITE DIAGRAM

Quick Write

Photosynthesis is an important process because it makes food + oxygen. Plants use light energy to convert water + carbon dioxide into glucose + oxygen. There are two stages of photosynthesis: the light reactions require light + the dark reactions do not use light.
Glucose is a sugar that plants can make into other kinds of sugars, starch fats or protein. The oxygen gas is released to the air.

Quick Draw

$6 CO_2 + 6H_2O$

light

chlorophyll

$C_6 H_{12} O_6 + 6 O_2$

$O - C - O +$

oxygen

$C_6H_{12}O_6$

Source: Anne Westwater.

Writing Across All Curriculum Areas

Opportunities for writing exist in all classes and at every grade level. Student journals are a rich source of information for the teacher, in addition to serving as vehicles for students' reflection while refining their thinking. Although free writing is valuable, there are times when the teacher may wish to add structure by asking the students to respond to questions or to complete sentences. Figure 10.3 shows some examples.

A secondary school French teacher uses writing in a unique manner in her two advanced classes: She has each class write anonymous love letters in French to students in the other class. She reports that this is one of her students' favorite activities and that their vocabulary increases dramatically, especially for adjec-

Student journals are a rich source of information for the teacher, in addition to serving as vehicles for students' reflection while refining their thinking.

~ Figure 10.3 ~
QUESTIONS OR SENTENCE STARTERS FOR JOURNAL WRITING

The one thing I'll remember about today's lesson is _____

I'm still confused about _____

What I'm finding hardest right now is _____

How does what I learned today fit with something I already know? _____

_____

What I understood today that I haven't understood before was _____

The problem in this lesson that was most difficult for me was _____

The activity I liked best today was _____

Explain the steps you used to solve a problem today:

    1. _____

    2. _____

    3. _____

    4: _____

A new insight or discovery for me was _____

tives. Two 5th grade teachers collaborate on a project in which students also exchange letters. In this activity, however, students in one class write "Dear Abby letters" to students in the other class. Students describe a classroom or playground problem and ask "Abby" how she thinks it should be solved. When the letters are received, students hold class discussions about possible solutions before they write their responses.

Teachers can adapt the well-known KWL (*Know*, *Want* to know, and *Learned*) tool as a writing strategy by instructing students to start a Reflection Journal at the beginning of a unit of study. They begin by writing what they think they know about a topic and add to that what they would like to know. As they progress through the unit, they can add their observations about what they are learning. These journals are excellent sources of discussion when students compare what they have written. Additionally, the teacher's periodic reading of student journals can be an excellent diagnostic tool for monitoring student thinking and adjusting instruction appropriately.

A secondary French teacher uses writing in a unique manner in her two advanced classes: She has each class write anonymous love letters in French to students in the other class.

Mnemonics as Tools to Aid Memory

How do you remember the number of days in a month, the order of the colors of the visible spectrum, or the names of the lines on the treble clef? You probably use a memory aid called a mnemonic device or strategy—a method for organizing information in a way that makes it more likely to be remembered. The term *mnemonic* comes from the Greek word *mnema*, meaning memory. Mnemonics have a long, rich history. Ancient Greeks used them extensively and considered mnemonics a true rigorous art requiring imagination, effort, and a good mind. They considered the study of mnemonics an essential element of a classical education. (This made sense in a culture where stone or clay tablets were the primary medium used for writing.)

Today, however, the topic of mnemonics is rarely discussed in educational journals or even among teachers. The reason for this avoidance is that, given the emphasis on learning through relevancy and meaningfulness, many teachers view mnemonics as mere memorization or "memory tricks." Many educators consider mnemonics as intellectually unrespectable because they do little to enhance meaningful understanding. The truth, however, is that mnemonics can be effective learning strategies. We can use them successfully to help students recall the meaning of terms, dates, and facts they need to know: foreign language vocabulary, scientific and mathematical terminology, music notation, the chronology of historical events, and factual information in many other subject areas. Contrary to what many people believe, mnemonic strategies do not foster simple rote memory at the expense of comprehension and problem solving. In fact, available research evidence suggests that using mnemonic strategies to acquire factual information can often improve students' ability to apply the information (Levin & Levin, 1990).

The ancient Greeks considered the study of mnemonics an essential element of a classical education.

Why Mnemonics Work

Mnemonics are based on the principle that the brain is a pattern-seeking device, always looking for associations between the information it is receiving and what is already stored. If the brain can find no link or association, it is highly unlikely that the information will be stored in long-term memory. Unfortunately, this scenario is relatively commonplace in the classroom. We require students to remember a considerable body of material that has little or no inherent meaning, such as letters of the alphabet or the items that make up a classification system. For these types of information, mnemonic strategies are extremely effective. They create links or associations that give the brain an organizational framework on which to hook new information. The process is relatively simple and consists of three basic steps:

Mnemonics are based on the principle that the brain is a pattern-seeking device, always looking for associations between the information it is receiving and what is already stored.

1. The student has—or is given—a framework.
2. New items are associated with the framework.
3. The known cues—the framework—aid in the recall of the new information.

For example, suppose the teacher wants her students to remember the order of the colors of the visible spectrum. Since there doesn't appear to be any reason the order is red, orange, yellow, green, blue, indigo, and violet, it would be difficult to remember. However, if the teacher introduces the students to a fictitious person, Roy G. Biv, and explains that the letters of his name each stand for the first letter of the colors in the spectrum, she provides a framework that makes the information easier to learn and more likely to be readily recalled. In this case, the teacher provided the students with the mnemonic framework. Later, students generate their own frameworks for other pieces of knowledge, which are often more meaningful and therefore more powerful as a memory tool.

Types of Mnemonic Strategies

Mnemonics encompass a broad range of categories, some more familiar than others. One of the most common is the acrostic sentence. If you took music lessons as a child, you probably learned the notes of the lines on the treble clef by repeating the sentence, "Every good boy does fine." The first letter of each word is the note on one of the lines, and the order of the sentence is the order of the lines from the bottom to the top of the staff. Other familiar acrostic sentences are "My very eager mother just served us nine pizzas," which gives the order of the planets from the sun outward (Mercury, Venus, Earth, Mars, Jupiter, Saturn, Uranus, Neptune, and Pluto); "In Persia, men are tall," for the stages of the cell cycle (interphase, prophase, metaphase, anaphase, telophase); "All hairy men will buy razors," for the constituents of soil (air, humus, mineral salts, water, bacteria, rock particles); and "Kids prefer cheese over fried green spinach," the zoological classifications in descending order (kingdom, phylum, class, order, family, genus, and species). One 2nd grade student explained to his teacher that the directions, north, east, south, and west, are easy to remember if you say, "Never eat slimy worms." Incidentally, if you'd like to remember how to spell mnemonics, you might remember that "Mnemonics neatly eliminate man's only nemesis, insufficient cerebral storage."

Acronyms are similar to acrostic sentences, except that they use single words rather than sentences. If students have difficulty remembering when to use "affect" versus "effect," they will probably benefit from the acronym RAVEN, which stands for "Remember affect (is a) verb, effect (is a) noun." The name "McHale" will help students remember the forms of energy: mechanical, chemical, heat, atomic, light, and electrical. An acronym for the names of the great lakes is HOMES: Huron, Ontario, Michigan, Erie, and Superior.

Many mnemonics take the form of rhymes and phrases. Probably the best-known rhymes are "I before E except after C, or when rhyming with A, as in neighbor and weigh" and "Thirty days hath September, April, June, and November." Most elementary teachers use the rhyme, "When two vowels go walking, the first one does the talking," to help students remember when a vowel is not pronounced. Many a chemistry student knows the rhyme, "May her rest be long and placid; she added water to acid. The other girl did what she oughter; she added acid to water." Reading Roman numerals is easier if you learned the rhyme, "X shall stand for playmates ten; V for five stalwart men; I for one as I'm alive; C for a hundred, D for five (hundred); M for a thousand soldiers true; and L for fifty, I'll tell you."

Mnemonic phrases are used primarily for assistance in remembering which spelling to use for homonyms or other words that are easily confused. To recall, for example, when to use "principle" versus "principal," students can be taught to remember that "The principal is your pal." Other phrases help with words often misused or misspelled, such as "Dessert is bigger in the middle, just like you'll be if you eat too much of it," or "Miss Pell never misspells," or "Stationery goes in envelopes," or "There's a rat in separate." An excellent resource for spelling and vocabulary mnemonics is *Vocabutoons (Vocabulary Cartoons)* by Sam Burchers (1997).

When you recall how powerful visuals are for storing and recalling information, it isn't surprising that they play a role in many mnemonic strategies. *Keyword mnemonics* comprise one of the few mnemonic strategies that have been the subject of numerous research studies. Using keywords involves associating two items using mental imagery and is often employed in the study of new vocabulary. For example, suppose you are taking a class in Spanish and need to memorize a vocabulary list by the next class. You could say the words over and over (rote rehearsal), hoping they eventually stick in your brain, or perhaps you might make flash cards with the Spanish word on one side and its English equivalent on the other, and use them to try to remember the meanings. If you had learned how to use keyword mnemonics, however, you would take each Spanish word and select a concrete noun in English that sounds like that word. For the word "carta" (letter), you might imagine a large grocery cart and picture a giant letter in the cart; or for the word "pato" (duck), you could picture a duck with a pot on its head.

Research on the keyword method, conducted by Pressley and Levin in 1978, produced impressive results. Using this strategy, 6th graders recalled twice as many foreign words as children of comparable age and ability who were left to learn the words on

When you recall how powerful visuals are for storing and recalling information, it isn't surprising that they play a role in many mnemonic strategies.

their own. Further research found that the keyword mnemonic strategy was successful when extended to other areas, such as abstract prose. When the investigators tested students after a period of time, they maintained their gains, suggesting that keyword mnemonic strategies have a lasting effect (Joyce & Showers, 1988; Pressley & Levin, 1978).

Loci mnemonics also use links or associations to create memory hooks, but rather than linking a word to an image, this strategy links words to physical locations that are already firmly established in memory. (*Loci* is Latin for "places.") Cicero and other orators of the Classical Era used this method to remember the content and order of their speeches. In loci mnemonics, you take a mental walk through a familiar place, such as your house, and visualize the items to be remembered in various locations in your house. As with all imagery, it helps to make the images vivid by exaggerating their size, making them animated, or changing their color. When you need to recall the list, you take another walk through the house and "see" the items in the order you placed them.

Narrative chaining is closely related to loci mnemonics and involves weaving items to be remembered into a story framework. As an example, groups of students in a civics class created a narrative to help them remember the freedoms listed in the First Amendments to the Constitution: the freedoms of religion, speech, the press, and assembly, and the right to bear arms. One narrative imagined a large group of people marching through the town and eventually assembling in front of a large cathedral. They strung cables, set up microphones, and began giving speeches about their right to have guns to protect themselves. Many members of the press arrived and began taking photographs and videotaping interviews with members of the group.

The narrative-chaining method has been shown to be far superior to ordinary rote memorization, in which subjects try to remember without aid. Researchers Bower and Clark instructed subjects to learn 12 different lists of 10 unrelated words. Some subjects made up a story linking together the words in each list. The students in the control group studied the words without the aid of this technique. Students who used the narrative-chaining mnemonic strategy later recalled more than 90 percent of the 120 words, whereas the control group remembered only 13 percent (McGee & Wilson, 1984).

Teaching Mnemonic Strategies

Research indicates that students' performance on memory tasks is related to age.

Research indicates that students' performance on memory tasks is related to age. Immature learners (including children with mental retardation and learning disabilities) are most likely to have problems with memory tasks and, therefore, to have a greater risk of experiencing learning difficulties (Pressley & Levin, 1987). Throughout the elementary school years, students progressively perform better on memory tests, but they do not spontaneously produce memory strategies at times when such strategies would be useful—until around age 10. At about 5th grade, students begin to demonstrate a more efficient use of memory strategies (Moely et al., 1969).

Researchers have also shown that higher-achieving students of all ages are more likely to be able to invent effective learning strategies on their own, whereas lower-achieving students or students with learning disabilities are less likely to do so. Immature students, however, and those who generally are not successful learners, can be taught to use efficient strategies through demonstration and numerous opportunities to practice. Even a common memory technique such as repeating information to yourself is probably learned by example rather than developed spontaneously. Where do children learn these skills? Evidence indicates that the classroom plays an important role (Moely et al., 1969). Teachers can help students understand how their memories work, demonstrate various mnemonic devices, and provide prompts for when to use these strategies. When students know appropriate strategies and how to use them, they are much more likely to make "informed" judgments about when to use them.

Active Rehearsal Strategies for Long-Term Retention

The discussion of working memory in Chapter 6 distinguished between rote and elaborative rehearsal. We saw that rote rehearsal is a productive method for acquiring certain skills or procedures and for attaining automaticity in them; for example, to become proficient at touch typing or throwing a softball, you have to practice the skills over and over. But for semantic memory, rote rehearsal is not effective or efficient. For semantic information, elaborative rehearsal is much more effective. The preceding chapters of this book presented many elaborative rehearsal strategies that work well for encoding and retrieving the enormous amount of information we teach in schools. You may have noticed that all these strategies actively involve the learner. This section examines additional strategies that allow students to actively process information.

The saying, "The best way to learn something is to teach it," contains more than a little truth.

Peer Teaching

The saying, "The best way to learn something is to teach it" contains more than a little truth. Teaching a concept or skill to someone else requires a fairly high level of understanding. Too often we check for students' understanding by asking them if they understand or if they have any questions. Though this might work in some situations, often students think they understand when they don't or are hesitant to admit they don't. Instead of asking these questions, a better method might be for the students to select a partner and decide which of them will be

"A" and which will be "B." After teaching a portion of the lesson, the teacher asks "A" to pretend that "B" was out of the room for the last few minutes and missed the instruction. "A" now has the job of teaching "B" the information that has just been covered. Later in the lesson, the roles are reversed. While the students are teaching each other, the teacher carefully monitors the students' explanations.

Peer teaching accomplishes several objectives. First, it allows the students an opportunity to rehearse what they have learned, thus strengthening their neural pathways. Also, students are likely to give more attention to the lesson knowing they'll be required to share the information. This approach also teaches the students mental organization: When "A" takes his turn to teach "B," it allows him to discover what he really understands and what is still unclear. Finally, peer teaching provides valuable diagnostic information for the teacher, who finds out how well students comprehend the material and what misconceptions they may have formed. It is much better to discover the misconceptions while you are teaching than to wait until a test to uncover them.

Peer teaching can be structured in various ways. Students can write a short summary or sketch a quick web of what they've learned before teaching each other; the teacher can instruct students to reflect on what they've learned for one minute before engaging in teaching (often called "Think, Pair, Share"); or student pairs can teach other pairs.

A secondary science teacher uses a modification of peer teaching that he calls "Double Check." He pairs students and gives them three to five minutes to accomplish two tasks. First, each student silently reads a paragraph in the text; then, with the book closed, he or she verbally summarizes the information while the partner checks the text for content accuracy. The partners take turns generating or answering each other's questions.

Active Review

Although a review of previously learned material is essential, it can be boring and unproductive, especially if the teacher takes full responsibility for the review. (Remember that the person doing the work is the one growing the dendrites.) Involving students in the process can increase the effectiveness of the review and is motivating and fun for students as well. After the first six weeks of school, a geometry teacher schedules reviews once a week throughout the school year. She does not conduct the reviews, however; her students do. The students are assigned a date, but they may choose any previous content they wish to review for the class. They complete a form indicating which content they have chosen, why they chose it, and what materials or props they will use. They also write a one-page description of their topic and their objectives for the teacher to approve. This teacher says that her students choose an amazing variety of presentation structures, from puppet shows to cartoons, quizzes, and mini-dramas. Best of all, she reports that the students' interest in and understanding of geometry has increased tremendously.

The person doing the work is the one growing the dendrites.

Games can provide an active, motivating way for students to review what they've learned, but their effectiveness is enhanced if the students participate in the design or construction of the game. One 6th grade teacher instructs student teams to design a game to review a social studies unit they had just completed. They brainstorm the qualities of a good game, develop a rubric from their brainstorming, and then create their games. Some teams constructed board games, others designed game shows. One day was set aside as "Review Day," and teams rotated through each game, providing multiple opportunities for rehearsal of the material.

Vocabulary review is more fun when the meanings of words are tested in a game format. One teacher uses a "Pictionary" type of game in which students draw pictures to represent their words and the other students try to determine the word and its meaning. Another class reviews vocabulary words for an upcoming test by acting them out in teams.

Hands-On Learning Activities

Would you rather go on a cruise to Hawaii or see slides of someone's trip there? Sounds like a pretty silly question, yet we have traditionally structured our students' learning by "showing them slides." We have placed students at desks, admonished them to be quiet, and limited their study of the curriculum to reading or hearing rather than experiencing. Aristotle supposedly said, "What we have to learn to do, we learn by doing." Concrete experience is one of the best ways to make strong, long-lasting neural connections. These experiences engage more of the senses and use multiple pathways to store—and therefore more ways to recall—information. This is probably why we remember what we have experienced much better than what we have heard or read. True, it is not possible for students to experience everything we want them to learn, but we probably miss many opportunities to engage students in more authentic learning.

In selecting or designing hands-on activities, it is important to emphasize that the purpose of these activities is to enhance learning within a rigorous, relevant curriculum. We may be tempted to read or hear about an activity that sounds like a lot of fun and to "insert" it into the day's agenda to add interest or motivation. While you might be able to justify the activity as helping students follow directions or work cooperatively in a group, the activity should serve a broader purpose. Remember that hands-on activities are extremely valuable as long as they are also "minds-on."

Elementary School. A study of birds and how they reproduce is enhanced by hatching chicken or duck eggs in an incubator.

Hands-on activities are extremely valuable as long as they are also "minds-on."

Additional ways for young children to learn are time lines for development, need for nutrients (both for the unborn bird and after hatching), and care of the baby birds after they have hatched. A follow-up unit could include how human activities affect birds. The activity mentioned earlier on how birds are affected by oil spills would fit well with this unit.

To begin a unit on fractions with elementary students, students can peel and section an orange, count the sections, and discuss the parts (fractions) of the whole. In a study of the human body, students are much more likely to understand the functions of the heart if they are shown how to measure their pulse while resting and then after running in place. A stethoscope and blood-pressure cuff can be used to further extend the learning. Partially inflating a balloon and squeezing the air from one end of the balloon to the other will help students understand the pressure of air in their lungs and introduce them to Boyle's Law (decreasing a gas's volume increases its pressure.)

Middle School. Well-structured, hands-on activities are ideal for high-energy adolescents. These students love activities that contain an element of surprise and that engage them in physical activity. For example, in a unit on measurement, students will be fascinated to discover that they are all approximately six feet tall (if they use their own feet as the measure). They can prove this by marking their head heights on paper taped to the wall then measuring their height by using a tracing of their feet. They can also construct graphs and determine averages as part of this activity.

Many of today's classrooms comprise students from various backgrounds and cultures. To increase their understanding of culture, students can create sacks of artifacts representing elements of their culture. Students then present their "culture sacks" to the class, explaining the significance of the items they contain.

Students will long remember the process of osmosis, which is vital in maintaining the water balance of living cells, if they use an egg with a dissolved shell as a model for the living cell membrane. They weigh two fresh eggs, then remove the shells by soaking the eggs overnight in vinegar. Students then place one egg into corn syrup and the other into distilled water for another 24 hours. On the third day, the difference in size, shape, and weight of the two eggs due to loss or uptake of water through the outer membrane (osmosis) is striking and unforgettable. Seeing is believing and understanding.

Secondary School. The concept of forces on structures is made clearer by a classic science activity that has many variations. Students are challenged to build the strongest structures they can with simple materials such as plastic straws, cellophane tape, and Popsicle sticks. It is important for students to record the building process they used, what principles they discovered, and how these principles apply equally to real structures. In this same vein, teachers could challenge students to build a brick wall (using 2-by-1-inch wooden blocks) strong enough to withstand a moderate earthquake. Teams of students brainstorm a system for the investigation, draw the pattern, build a segment of the wall, then compare their designs to those of other teams, noting the number of bricks needed, which walls are most likely to withstand the quake, etc.

Many physics teachers believe that their subject is best learned through hands-on activities. In these classrooms, you will see mini-lectures combined with groups of students involved in activities such as measuring densities with self-built hydrometers, or testing basic physics concepts of force and friction with small cars on an intricate model of tracks they have built.

Hands-on activities generate energy and enthusiasm about the subject by getting students to interact with and learn from one another. These activities require careful planning, organization, resources, and often a good deal of creativity on the part of

Hands-on activities generate enthusiasm and energy about the subject by getting students to interact with and learn from one another.

the teacher, but teachers report that the pay-off for student learning is worth it.

Conclusion

We've now reached the end of our journey through the brain, or it might be more accurate to say that we've just begun our journey. During the past three decades, we've learned more about the brain than in all of recorded history, but there is much more to learn. As exciting as the new developments in neuroscience are, the dialogue that has begun between neuroscientists, cognitive scientists, and educators is even more exciting. For the first time, we're seeing substantive conversations between those who are conducting the research and educators who are looking for applications of the research. Our challenge is to continue to read, study, and become informed consumers. Information about the brain and how it learns is not merely interesting, it's an essential element in the foundation on which we should base our educational decisions. The brain matters because our children matter.

Synapse Strengtheners

1. Select one of the writing activities to use with your students. Keep your own written record containing a description of the activity, students' reactions, problems encountered, and your assessment of its effectiveness.

2. Prepare a short presentation, to be given at a faculty meeting, explaining what mnemonics are, why they work, and when it would be appropriate to use them. Schedule a follow-up session for teachers to share mnemonics they or their students have created.

3. If your study group has started a booklet of brain-compatible strategies, add examples of writing activities, mnemonics, and other active learning strategies.

Glossary

Acetylcholine—A neurotransmitter found in the brain, spinal cord, neuromuscular junction, and autonomic nervous system.

Action Potential—The nerve impulse that is conducted down the axon to transmit information to other neurons.

Adrenalin—A neurotransmitter synthesized from norepinephrin, also called ephinephrin.

Agnosia—Loss of the ability to name or interpret what is seen.

Agonist—A drug that activates a particular receptor; the opposite of antagonist.

Agraphia—Loss or lessened ability to write.

Alexia—The inability to recognize and name written words.

Amygdala—A nucleus of cells located at the base of the temporal lobe (in the basal ganglia) believed to be the source of emotions and emotional memory.

Anomia—The inability to verbalize the names of people, objects, and places.

Anosognosia—The denial of loss of a capacity, such as the denial of paralysis after a stroke.

Antagonist—A drug that blocks a particular receptor; opposite of agonist.

Aphasia—The loss or lessened ability to produce speech.

Apraxia—The inability to make purposeful movements despite normal muscles and coordination.

Astrocytes—Glial cells involved in nutritive support for neurons. Also called astroglia.

Autism—A condition usually appearing in early childhood characterized by abnormal social interaction, resistance to physical or eye contact, and lack of communication.

Autonomic Nervous System—Located outside the brain and spinal cord, obtains information from internal organs and provides output to them.

Axon—A long fiber emerging from a neuron that carries nerve impulses to other neurons.

Axon Terminal—The ending of an axon branch that connects to the neural target. Also called the terminal bouton or the presynaptic terminal.

Blood-Brain Barrier (BBB)—A filtering system of glial cells that keeps many substances out of the brain.

Brainstem—A structure just above the spinal cord that allows the brain to communicate with the spinal cord and peripheral nerves and controls, among other functions, respiration and heartbeat.

Broca's Area—The central region for the production of speech, typically located in the left hemisphere.

Carotid Artery—Any of the four main arteries located in the neck and head that supply the brain with blood.

Central Nervous System (CNS)—The collective term for the brain and spinal cord, which receive sensory information from all the sensory organs in the body and trigger appropriate motor responses.

Cerebellum—A two-lobed structure overlying the top of the brain stem that helps control coordination, balance, and some aspects of motor learning

Cerebral Cortex—The deeply folded outer layer of the cerebral hemispheres (the gray matter) that is responsible for perception, awareness of emotion, planning, and conscious thought. Also called the neocortex.

Cerebrospinal Fluid (CSF)—A clear fluid found in the ventricles in the brain, the protective covering (meninges) of the brain, and in the spinal cord.

Computerized Axial Tomography (CAT)—A technique that uses a computer and x-rays to produce a cross-sectional picture of tissue.

Consolidation—The process by which memories are moved from temporary storage in the hippocampus to more permanent storage in the cortex.

Corpus Callosum—A large bundle of myelinated axons that connects the left and right cerebral hemispheres.

Cortisol—A steroid hormone that mobilizes energy stores, suppresses the immune system, and has direct actions on some central nervous system neurons.

Dendrite—The branched extension from the cell body that receives information from other neurons.

Dendritic Spine—Small extensions on dendrites that are often the site of a synapse.

Dopamine—A neurotransmitter found in many areas of the brain and having multiple functions depending on where it acts. Important for movement and is thought to regulate emotional responses.

Electroconvulsive Therapy (ECT)—An electric shock applied to the brain to induce seizures; used in some cases of severe depression.

Electroencephalogram (EEG)—A recorded tracing of electrical brain activity (brain waves) obtained through electrodes placed on the skull.

Endorphins—Neurotransmitters (opioid peptides) produced in the brain that generate cellular and behavioral effects like those of morphine.

Epinephrine—A neurotransmitter synthesized from norepinephrine and acting with it to activate the autonomic nervous system. Also called adrenalin.

Fetal Alcohol Syndrome (FAS)—A condition in which a mother's consumption of alcohol produces a range of physical and mental characteristics in the developing fetus.

Frontal Lobe—One of the four major divisions of each hemisphere of the cerebral cortex located in the most anterior (front) part of the brain and responsible for higher-level cognition.

Functional Magnetic Resonance Imaging (fMRI)—A technique for imaging brain structure and activity by measuring oxygen use in the brain.

Gamma-Amino Butyric Acid (GABA)—A neurotransmitter synthesized from glutamate, whose primary function is to inhibit the firing of neurons.

Glial Cell (Neuroglia)—The most common cell in the nervous system. It plays various roles in support and protection of neurons.

Glutamate—A neurotransmitter that acts primarily to excite neurons.

Habituation—A process by which a nerve cell adapts to an initially novel stimulus and decreases behavioral responses to repeated stimulation.

Hebb Synapse—A synapse that increases in strength when both the presynaptic and postsynaptic neurons are active at the same time.

Hippocampus—A structure near the center of the brain deep within the temporal lobe in each hemisphere that plays an important role in declarative memory storage and retrieval.

Homeostasis—The balanced functioning of physiological processes and maintenance of the body's constant internal environment.

Hypothalamus—A structure near the center of the brain in each hemisphere that controls body temperature, heart rate, hunger, thirst, sex drive, aggressive behavior, and pleasure, and is responsible for the responses to the stress response.

Ion—A charged atom, the most common of which in the brain are sodium, potassium, calcium, and chloride.

Ion Channel—A protein that lies in the cell membrane that allows ions to pass from one side of the membrane to the other.

Limbic System—An older term referring to a group of brain structures that regulate emotions.

Long-Term Potentiation (LTP)—A persistent strengthening of synaptic strength that occurs with repeated activation of the synapse and may be the analog of the Hebb synapse.

Magnetic Resonance Imaging (MRI)—A technique for imaging soft tissue in the brain, using magnets and radio waves.

Medial Temporal Lobe (MTL)—An area of the brain that houses the hippocampus and is critical to the formation of memory.

Mitochondria—Small organelles inside the cell body that provide energy for the cell by converting sugar and oxygen into special energy molecules.

Motor Cortex—The lateral part of the frontal lobes that extends from ear to ear across the roof of the brain. It governs movement.

Myelin—A sheath of fatty tissue that forms an insulating cover around some axons; it permits faster conduction of the action potential. The layer is formed by Schwann cells in the peripheral nervous system and oligodendrocytes in the central nervous system.

Neuron—The principal information-carrying cellular unit of the nervous system generally consisting of a cell body (soma), dendrites, and an axon.

Neuropeptides—Peptides (short sequences of amino acids) that serve as neurotransmitters.

Neurotransmitter—A chemical released by neurons that crosses the synapse, allowing communication between one neuron and another.

Norepinephrine—A neurotransmitter synthesized from dopamine; it is involved in arousal, reward, and regulation of mood. Also known as noradrenalin.

Nucleus Accumbens—A structure in the middle of the brain that has large numbers of dopamine receptors and is central to the reward system pathway.

Occipital Lobe—One of the four major divisions of each hemisphere of the cerebral cortex, located in the back of brain and responsible for the processing of visual stimuli.

Oligodendrocyte—A glial cell that provides myelin in the central nervous system.

Parietal Lobes—One of the four major divisions of each hemisphere of the cerebral cortex, located in the upper back part of the brain (between the occipital and frontal lobes), with responsibility for sensory integration.

Peripheral Nervous System (PNS)—Located outside the brain and spinal cord, it carries information from the body to the CNS and provides motor output to the muscles that allow us to move. It includes the autonomic nervous system (ANS).

Pineal Gland—An endocrine organ in the center of the brain responsible for secreting the hormone melatonin, which is responsible for regulating circadian rhythms.

Plasticity—Changes in neural connectivity.

Positron Emission Tomography (PET)—A technique for imaging physiological activity in the brain, using radioactive dyes injected into the bloodstream.

Postsynaptic Neuron—The neuron that receives the neurotransmitters released by the presynaptic neuron.

Presynaptic Neuron—The neuron that releases the neurotransmitters into the synapse.

Prosopagnosia—A neurological condition in which specific faces can't be recognized.

Rapid Eye Movement Sleep (REM Sleep)—A type of sleep characterized by a decreased muscle tone and an increase in rapid eye movement, electrical activity, and deep dreaming.

Receptor—A site on a cell membrane where a neurotransmitter can bind. Most receptors are highly selective and will only bind a particular neurotransmitter.

Reticular Activating System (RAS)—A system of nerve pathways in the brainstem concerned with levels of arousal from hypervigilance to drowsiness.

Reuptake—A process by which released neurotransmitters are absorbed for subsequent reuse.

Serotonin—A neurotransmitter believed to play a role in temperature regulation, sensory perception, mood, and sleep. A number of antidepressant drugs are targeted to brain serotonin systems.

Somatosensory Cortex—A part of the cortex just behind the motor cortex that receives information through the sensory organs.

Spinal Cord—A large bundle of fibers of the CNS (beginning at the base of the brainstem and continuing down to the tailbone), which serves motor and sensory functions.

Stimulus—A maneuver that can activate a sensory receptor.

Synapse—The physical structure that makes an electrochemical connection between a sending (presynaptic) neuron and a receiving (postsynaptic) neuron.

Synaptic Cleft—The gap separating two neurons at the synapse.

Temporal Lobe—One of the four major divisions of each hemisphere of the cerebral cortex located on the lower part of the brain near the ears and responsible for auditory processing and some aspects of memory.

Terminal—The end of an axon branch.

Thalamus—A large collection of cells that relays all sensory information (except smell) to the appropriate part of the cortex for processing.

Ventricles—Four fluid-filled (cerebrospinal fluid) cavities in the brain.

Vesicle—A membrane-enclosed structure (organelle) containing neurotransmitters and found in the axon terminal.

Wernicke's Area—The language center responsible for the syntax and comprehension of speech (typically in the left hemisphere).

References and Bibliography

Ackerman, S. (1992). *Discovering the brain*. Washington, DC: National Academy Press.

Amaral, D. (2000, May 6). *Memory and the brain: The hippocampus at work*. From a speech given at the Spring 2000 Symposium on Brain Research: Implications for Teaching and Learning, San Diego, California.

Amaral, D., & Soltesz, I. (1997). Hippocampal formation. *Encyclopedia of human biology* (2nd ed., Vol. 4). New York: Academic Press.

Atkinson, R., & Raugh, M. R. (1975). An application of the mnemonic keyword method to the acquisition of a Russian vocabulary. *Journal of Experimental Psychology: Human Learning and Memory, 104*, 126–133.

Bahrick, H. P., Bahrick, P. O., & Wittlinger, R. P. (1976). Fifty years of memory for names and faces: A cross-sectional approach. *Journal of Experimental Psychology: General, 104*, 54–75.

Bear, M. F., Conners, B. W., & Paradiso, M. A. (1996). *Neuroscience: Exploring the brain*. New York: Lippincott, Williams & Wilkins.

Binney, R., & Janson, M. (Eds.) (1990). *Atlas of the mind and body*. London: Mitchell Beazley Publishers.

Blood, A. J., Aztorre, R. J., Bermudez, T., & Evans, A. C. (1999). Emotional responses to pleasant and unpleasant music correlate with activity in para-limbic brain regions. *Nature Neuroscience, 2*, 382–387.

Bloom, B. (1986, February). Automaticity, the hands and feet of genius. *Educational Leadership, 43*(5), 70–77.

Borne, R. (1994). *Serotonin: The neurotransmitter for the 90s*. [Online article]. Available: http://www.fairlite.com/ocd/articles/ser90.shtml.

Brandt, R. (1998). *Powerful learning*. Alexandria, VA: Association for Supervision and Curriculum Development.

Brashers-Krug, T., Shadmehr, R., & Bizzi, E. (1996, July). Consolidation in human motor memory. *Nature, 382*, 252–255.

Bull, B. L., & Wittrock, M. C. (1973). Imagery in the learning of verbal definitions. *British Journal of Educational Psychology, 43*, 289–293.

Burchers, S. (1997). *Vocabutoons: Vocabulary cartoons*. Punta Gorda, FL: New Monic Books.

Cahill, L. (2000, January 19). *Emotions and memory.* From a speech given at the Learning Brain Expo, San Diego, California.

Carter, R. (1998). *Mapping the mind.* Los Angeles: University of California Press.

Center for Problem-Based Learning. (2001). *About the Center for Problem-Based Learning.* [Online]. Aurora, IL: Illinois Mathematics and Science Academy. Available: http://www.imsa.edu/team/cpbl/center.html

Chase, W., & Simon, H. (1973). Perception in chess. *Cognitive Psychology, 1,* 33–81.

Cherry, E. C. (1953). Some experiments on the recognition of speech. *Journal of the Acoustical Society of America, 25,* 975–979.

Chudler, E. (2001). *Neuroscience for kids.* [Online]. Seattle: University of Washington. Available: http://faculty.washington.edu/chudler/neurok.html

Countryman, J. (1992). *Writing to learn mathematics: Strategies that work, K–12.* Portsmouth, NH: Heinemann Educational Books.

Cowan, W. M. (1979). The development of the brain. *Scientific American, 241*(3), 106–117.

Crick, F. (1994). *The astonishing hypothesis: The scientific search for the soul.* New York: Charles Scribner's Sons.

Damasio, A. (1994). *Descartes' error: Emotion, reason, and the human brain.* New York: G. P. Putnam's Sons.

D'Aracangelo, M. (1999, October). Learning about learning to read: A conversation with Sally Shaywitz. *Educational Leadership, 57*(2), 26–31.

Davis, J. (1997). *Mapping the mind: The secrets of the human brain and how it works.* Secaucus, NJ: Carol Publishing Group.

Delisle, R. (1997). *How to use problem-based learning in the classroom.* Alexandria, VA: Association for Supervision and Curriculum Development.

Dewey, J. (1937). *Experience in education.* New York: Macmillan.

Diamond, M. C. (1988). *Enriching heredity: The impact of the environment on the anatomy of the brain.* New York: Free Press.

Diamond, M., Hopson, J., & Diamond, M. C. (1998). *Magic trees of the mind: How to nurture your child's intelligence, creativity, and healthy emotions from birth through adolescence.* New York: E. P. Dutton.

Evans, A. (1996, May). Addressing TV violence in the classroom. *Phi Delta Kappa Research Bulletin, 16,* 1–4.

Fajardo, M., Florido, J., Villaverde, C., Oltras, C., Gonzales-Ramirez, A., & Gonzalez-Gomez, F. (1994, June 15). Plasma levels of beta-endorphin and ACTH during labor and immediate puerperium. *European Journal of Obstetrics, Gynecology, and Reproductive Biology, 55*(2), 105–108.

Gazzaniga, M. (1997). *Conversations in the neurosciences.* Cambridge, MA: Massachusetts Institute of Technology Press.

Gazzaniga, M. (1998). *The mind's past.* Berkeley, CA: University of California Press.

Gazzaniga, M., Bogen, J., & Sperry, R. (1962). Some functional effects of sectioning the cerebral commissures in man. *Proceedings of the National Academy of Science, USA, 48,* 1765–1769.

Gazzaniga, M., Ivry, R., & Mangun, R. (1998). *Cognitive neuroscience.* New York: W. W. Norton.

Goodlad, J. (1984). *A place called school.* New York: McGraw-Hill.

Gould, E., Reeves, A., Graziano, M., & Gross, C. (1999). Neurogenesis in the neocoretex of adult primates. *Science, 286,* 548–552.

Grandin, T. (1995). *Thinking in pictures*. New York: Doubleday.

Greenfield, S. A. (1996). *The human mind explained*. New York: Henry Holt.

Greenfield, S. A. (1997). *The human brain: A guided tour*. New York: Basic Books.

Gregory, R. (Ed.) (1987). *The Oxford companion to the mind*. New York: Oxford University Press.

Hart, L. (1983). *Human brain, human learning*. New York: Longman.

Hilt, P. J. (1995). *Memory's ghost*. New York: Simon & Schuster.

Hobson, J. A. (1989). *Sleep*. New York: Scientific American Library.

Hoetker, K., & Ahlbrand, W. (1964). The persistence of the recitation. *American Educational Research Journal, 6,* 145–167.

Hooper, J., & Teresi, D. (1986). *The 3-pound universe*. New York: Dell.

Hunt, M. (1982). *The universe within: A new science explores the human mind*. New York: Simon & Schuster.

Hyerle, D. (2000). *A field guide to using visual tools*. Alexandria, VA: Association for Supervision and Curriculum Development.

Joyce, B., & Showers, B. (1988). *Student achievement through staff development*. New York: Longman.

Kempermann, G., & Gage, F. (1999, May). New nerve cells for the adult brain. *Scientific American, 280*(6), 48–53.

Krumhansl, C. L., & Jusczyk, P. W. (1996, September). Infants' perception of phrase structure in music. *Psychological Science, 1,* 70–73.

Kotulak, R. (1996). *Inside the brain: Revolutionary discoveries of how the mind works*. Kansas City: Andrew McMeel.

LeDoux, J. (1996). *The emotional brain*. New York: Simon & Schuster.

Levin, M. E., & Levin, J. R. (1990). Scientific mnemonomies: Methods for maximising more than memory. *American Educational Research Journal, 27,* 301–321.

Levinthal, C. F. (1988). *Messengers of paradise: Opiates and the brain*. New York: Anchor Press/Doubleday.

Loftus, G. R., & Loftus, E. F. (1975). *Human memory: The processing of information*. New York: Halsted Press.

McGee, M. G., & Wilson, D. W. (1984). *Psychology: Science and application*. New York: West.

Miller, G. A. (1956). The magical number seven, plus or minus two: Some limits on our capacity for processing information. *Psychological Review, 63,* 81–97.

Moely, B. E., Olson, F. A., Halwes, T. G., & Flavell, J. H. (1969). Production deficiency in young children's clustered recall. *Developmental Psychology, 1,* 26–34.

Moyers, B. (1993). *Healing and the mind*. New York: Doubleday.

National Institute of Mental Health. (1997). *FMRI reveals dynamics of working memory*. [Online Press Release]. Washington, DC: National Institutes of Health. Available: http://www.nimh.nih.gov/events/prfmri.htm

National Institute of Mental Health. (1998). *Spatial short-term memory pinpointed in human brain*. [Online Press Release]. Washington, DC: National Institutes of Health. Available: http://www.nimh.nih.gov/events/prwmem.htm

National Research Council. (1999). *How people learn: Brain, mind, experience, and school*. Washington, DC: National Academy Press.

Brain
Matters: Translating Research into Classroom Practice

Olsen, K. (1995). *Science continuum of concepts for grades K–6.* Kent, WA: Center for the Future of Public Education.

Ornstein, R. (1998). *Psychology: The study of human experience* (2nd ed.). San Diego, CA: Harcourt Brace Jovanovich.

Ornstein, R. (1997). *The right mind.* Orlando, FL: Harcourt Brace.

Pascual-Leon, J. (1970). A maturational model for the transition rule in Piaget's developmental stages. *Acta Psychologica, 32,* 301–345.

Perkins, D. (1992). *Smart schools: From training memories to educating minds.* New York: The Free Press.

Pert, C. (1997). *Molecules of emotion.* New York: Scribner.

Posner, M. I., & Raichle, M. E. (1997). *Images of mind.* New York: Scientific American Library.

Pressley, M., & Levin, J. R. (1978). Developmental constraints associated with children's use of the keyword method of foreign language vocabulary learning. *Journal of Experimental Child Psychology, 26,* 359–372.

Pressley, M., & Levin, J. R. (1987). Elaborative learning strategies for the inefficient learner. In S. J. Ceci (Ed.), *Handbook of cognitive, social and neuropsychological aspects of learning disabilities* (Vol. 2, pp. 175–212). Hillsdale, NJ: Erlbaum.

Raugh, M. R., & Atkinson, R. C. (1975). A mnemonic method for learning a second-language vocabulary. *Journal of Educational Psychology, 67,* 1–16.

Restak, R. (1994). *Receptors.* New York: Bantam Books.

Sapolsky, R. (1994). *Why zebras don't get ulcers.* New York: W. H. Freeman & Company.

Schacter, D. (1996). *Searching for memory: The brain, the mind, and the past.* New York: Basic Books.

Scheibel, A. (2000, May 6). *A journey through the development of the human brain.* From a speech given at the Spring 2000 Symposium on Brain Research: Implications for Teaching and Learning, Berkeley, California.

Shaw, G. (2000). *Keeping Mozart in mind.* San Diego, CA: Academic Press.

Siegel, D. J. (1999). *The developing mind: Toward a neurobiology of interpersonal experience.* New York: Guilford Press.

Siegel, D. J. (2000, January 18). *The developing mind.* From a speech given at the Learning Brain Expo, San Diego, California.

Sirotnik, K. (1983). What you see is what you get: Consistency, persistence, and mediocrity in classrooms. *Harvard Educational Review, 53*(1), 16–31.

Squire, L. R., & Kandel, E. R. (2000). *Memory from mind to molecules.* New York: Scientific American Library.

Standing, L. (1973). Learning 10,000 pictures. *Quarterly Journal of Experimental Psychology, 25,* 207B222.

Sylwester, R. (1995). *A celebration of neurons: An educator's guide to the human brain.* Alexandria, VA: Association for Supervision and Curriculum Development.

Tallal, P. (2000). Experimental studies of language learning impairments: From research to remediation. In D. V. M. Bishop & L. B. Leonard (Eds.), *Speech and language impairments in children: Causes, characteristics, intervention, and outcome.* Hove, UK: Psychology Press.

Teachers' Curriculum Institute. (1999). *History alive! Engaging all learners in the diverse classroom* (2nd ed.). Mountain View, CA: Author.

Thach, W. T. (1996). On the specific role of the cerebellum in motor learning and cognition: Clues from PET activation and lesion studies in man. *Behavioral and Brain Sciences, 19,* 411–431.

Thompson, R. (1985). *The brain: An introduction to neuroscience.* New York: W. H. Freeman.

Torgesen, J. K. (1996). A model of memory from an information processing perspective: The special case of phonological memory. In G. R. Lyon & N. A. Krasnegor, N. A. (Eds.), *Attention, memory, and executive function* (pp. 157–184). Baltimore: Paul H. Brookes.

Torp, L., & Sage, S. (1998). *Problems as possibilities: Problem-based learning for K–12 education.* Alexandria, VA: Association for Supervision and Curriculum Development.

Towse, J. N., Hitch, G. J., & Hutton, U. (1998, August). A reevaluation of working memory capacity in children. *Journal of memory and language, 39*(2), 195–217.

Underwood, B. J. (1968). Forgetting. *Scientific American, 5*(228).

Wagner, R. (1996). From simple structure to complex function: Major trends in the development of theories, models, and measurements of memory. In G. R. Lyon & N. A. Krasnegor, N. A. (Eds.), *Attention, memory, and executive function* (pp. 139–156). Baltimore: Paul H. Brookes.

Index

About the Author

Patricia Wolfe is an independent consultant who speaks to educators and parents in schools across the United States and in international schools. Her professional background includes work as a public school teacher at all levels; staff development trainer for the Upland (California) School District; Director of Instruction for the Napa County Office of Education, Napa, California; and lead trainer for the International Principal Training Center in Rome and London. Her staff development experience includes conducting workshops for educators in Madeline Hunter's Elements of Effective Teaching and Clinical Supervision, Anthony Gregorc's Mind Styles, Carolyn Evertson's Classroom Management and Organization, and Peer Coaching. She has been featured in a number of ASCD and National Staff Development Council (NSDC) videotape productions and satellite broadcasts.

Wolfe's major interest over the past 15 years has centered on the educational implications and applications of current neuroscience, cognitive science, and educational research for teaching and learning. She can be reached at Mind Matters, Inc., 555 Randolph Street, Napa, CA 94559; phone and fax: (707) 226-1777; Web site: www.patwolfe.com; e-mail address: wolfe@napanet.net.

Related ASCD Resources: The Brain and Learning

Audiotapes

Achieving Major Goals with Brain-Based Learning, by Joan Caulfield and Wayne Jennings (#200173)

Emotion/Attention: Our Brain's Doorway to Reason and Logic, by Robert Sylwester, (#200114)

A Healthy Brain in the Learning Process, by Deborah G. Estes (#200156)

How Can Educators Use Knowledge About the Human Brain to Improve School Learning? by Eric Jensen, Renate Nummela Caine, and Robert Sylwester (#200096)

Translating Brain Research into Educational Practice-3 tapes Live Satellite Broadcasts by Pat Wolfe (#297154)

CD-ROM and Multimedia

Exploring Our Multiple Intelligences CD-ROM, (#596276)

The Human Brain Professional Inquiry Kit, by Bonnie Benesh (#99900)

Online Resources

Visit ASCD's Web site (www.ascd.org) for the following professional development opportunities:

Online Tutorials: *The Brain and Learning; Performance Assessments* (http://www.ascd.org/frametutorials.html)

Professional Development Online: *The Brain* (http://www.ascd.org/framepdonline.html) (for a small fee; password protected)

Print Products

Arts with the Brain in Mind by Eric Jensen (#101011)

ASCD Topic Pack: *Brain-Based Learning Topic Pack* (#197194)

A Celebration of Neurons: An Educator's Guide to the Human Brain by Robert Sylwester (#195085)

Dimensions of Learning Teachers' Manual, 2nd Edition (#197133) by Robert J. Marzano, Debra Pickering, and others

A Field Guide to Using Visual Tools, by David Hyerle (#100023)

Learning and Memory: The Brain in Action, by Marilee Sprenger (#199213)

Powerful Learning, by Ron Brandt (#198179)

Teaching with the Brain in Mind, by Eric Jensen (#198019)

Unleashing the Power of Perceptual Change: The Potential of Brain-Based Teaching, by Renate Nummela Caine and Geoffrey Caine, (#197170)

Videotapes

The Brain and Early Childhood (two tapes, #400054).

The Brain and Learning (four tapes, #498062).

The Brain and Mathematics Series (two tapes, #400237)

The Brain and Reading (three tapes, #499207).

For additional information, visit us on the World Wide Web (http://www.ascd.org), send an e-mail message to member@ascd.org, call the ASCD Service Center (1-800-933-ASCD or 703-578-9600, then press 2), send a fax to 703-575-5400, or write to Information Services, ASCD, 1703 N. Beauregard St., Alexandria, VA 22311-1714 USA.